CIY

[CROCHET-IT-YOURSELF]

15 Modern Crochet Designs to Stitch and Wear

Emma Wright

Photography by Kim Lightbody

Hardie Grant

QUADRILLE

CONTENTS

INTRODUCTION

I taught myself to crochet in the six weeks of holiday between my first and second years of college, after falling back in love with hand knitting. I spent hour after hour looking through old crochet books and delving deep into the thousands of online tutorials. After graduating in fashion knitwear and knitted textiles, I knew crochet would play an important role in my career. My first ever make was a simple bunny for my younger sister, followed by anything I could make out of a granny square: purses, hats and even dresses. I've since worked with many yarn brands and magazines to create modern but timeless crochet collections.

For me, crochet allows you a freedom that no other craft can. You can build and craft your fabric in any direction, keeping things classic or going freeform to create something artistic and three-dimensional. There's something so satisfying and soothing about the repetition of creating each individual stitch with just a hook and ball of yarn; the possibilities are endless. I'm a strong believer that every pattern is just a guide and it's what you add to that guide that makes that project personal, what makes it your own. That may begin with your yarn choice —the fiber, color or texture—followed by your choice of stitch, placement, color blocking or adding other elements such as zippers or embroidery. All these things bring personality and individuality to your projects, making them one of a kind.

Something I was keen to feature to this book was accessories; I wanted to include the classics such as a beanie hat, heeled socks, a chunky scarf and a backpack. I find designing accessories so much fun—you can easily add your own personality through color placement, construction or even through embroidery. I often get carried away swatching for accessories and, before I know it, I have the finished piece. After swatching, I use my final gauge (tension) for that design to calculate all the measurements I need for the finished sweater, cardigan or accessory. I then write the pattern and send it out to one of the lovely ladies who make them up for me—or if I'm lucky I might be able to make it up myself, depending on my other workload.

The garment projects in this book are classic, timeless and staple pieces to add to your repertoire. My hope for these projects is that, as well as introducing you to some new and practical techniques, they will also bring longevity to the pieces in your wardrobe. Having a classic sweater, cardigan—or even both—is a must for a capsule wardrobe and I hope you enjoy using my book to help you achieve both a 'CIY' collection whilst perfecting some new techniques along the way!

HOW TO USE THIS BOOK

Welcome to my crochet workshop: my aim for this book is to help you advance your crochet skills. I'm assuming you already know how to crochet and already have a couple of projects under your belt; there is no better way to learn than to 'Crochet It Yourself'. This book is split into three sections—Sweaters, Cardigans and Accessories—with each pattern containing its own CIY technique for you to master. Each pattern comes with helpful hints and tips and there are blank illustrations on pages 154–155 for you to draw out your own design ideas.

Design Process

Although I love craft, in any form, I like my designs to have a polished and modern finish. There is something so satisfying about creating those refined details by hand or hook. This is important to me when designing a new piece and often where my design process begins. I'm also an avid Pinterest scroller and create a new board for every new project I begin. You could also create a photo album on your phone, full of images you've taken from shopping on the high street, from magazines, books or catalogs, of flowers, architecture or art that makes you feel inspired. This can help with decisions on finishing, color choices and even what yarn you decide to use.

Using Color

When designing I often start with color. Working with color can be approached in many different ways—if you love it then why not wear it? You can find color inspiration and color trends anywhere; you can take inspiration from fashion, nature, art, photography. I enjoy going out for a walk and taking photos of surrounding landscapes and flowers for my color inspiration. I often add these images to my project mood boards. Beginning with primary colors is a great place to start, then introduce secondary and tertiary color to create your palette.

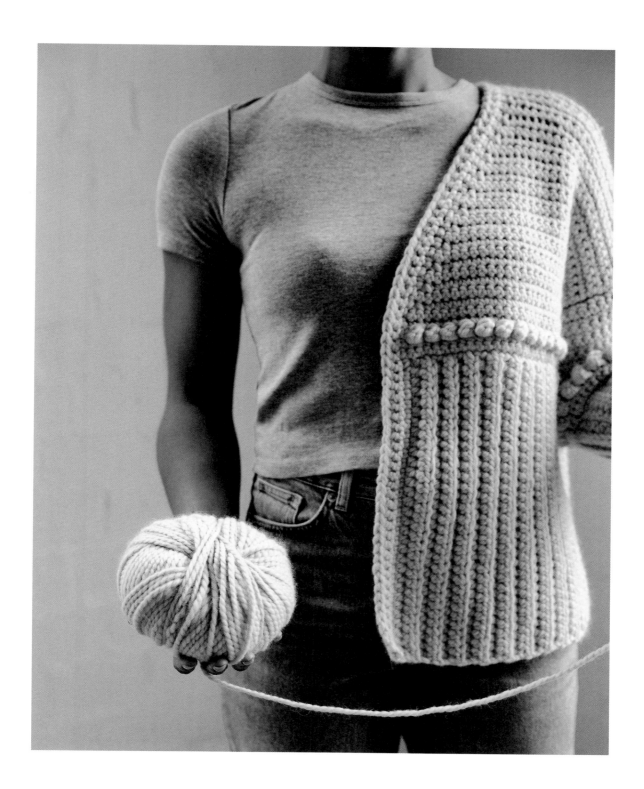

Working with complementary colors or following color trends can also give you a starting point. I like to start with a base color, something neutral such as white, cream, beige or black—and personally I would also class gray and navy as a base or background color. The mood of your palette will change depending on your base color; white will give you a fresher look, compared to black or gray, which will create a much moodier tone. Another great tip for creating a harmonious color palette is to work in odd numbers, so pick a palette of three, five or seven colors, especially if you are using this palette for color work.

Swatching

Once you have your inspiration and have put your mood board together—whether that's using paper and glue or digitally—it's time to start swatching. This is my favorite part of design; it's time to visit your bricks-and-mortar store, squish some yarn, pick up your favorite hook and get crocheting! Swatching is so important; although many find this part of starting a new project tedious, it's super important to get your gauge (tension) to match that given in the pattern otherwise the fit and size of your project may be incorrect. It's important to adjust your hook size to obtain the correct tension given in the pattern: if your swatch works up too big using the hook size in the pattern try a smaller hook, or if it is too small switch to a larger one. This way the finished fabric won't become too tight or loose.

Project Construction

Making up your project can be done in many ways. You can keep it simple and use running or back stitch, make things a little neater with mattress stitch or even crochet your work together using slip stitch or single crochet stitch. Crocheting your work together is quick and can be beneficial if you want a sturdy seam, when constructing accessories such as a backpack or a clutch purse. Coming from a pattern-cutting background I believe seams are there for a reason; we need them to help shape a garment or accessory and the type of sewing up we choose can play a big part in how that finished piece looks. I like to block each garment/accessory panel before and after construction. Blocking each piece before sewing can make construction easier and blocking after will help flatten out and soften each seam.

Aftercare

When you have invested time and money into your crochet you will want to make sure you look after it well. My advice would be to wash the items as few times as you can. I like to air my pieces outside on the washing line to freshen them up and make it possible to go longer between washing. If, however, you do need to launder them always follow the washing instructions from the ball band of the yarn you've used—it's a good idea to take a photo of these instructions on your phone or tablet. It's usually best to hand wash your crochet and keep light and dark colors separate. Use warm water and mix it with a gentle detergent. Submerge the garment or accessory and soak it for 10–15 minutes. Carefully rinse in warm water, then press out or squeeze to remove as much water as possible. Place flat on a dry towel, pulling it gently back into shape if necessary. Keep it away from sunlight and let it air dry at room temperature. Make sure the item is completely dry before putting it away. To store your crochet between wearing it's best to fold garments flat and not hang them; this avoids them stretching out of shape.

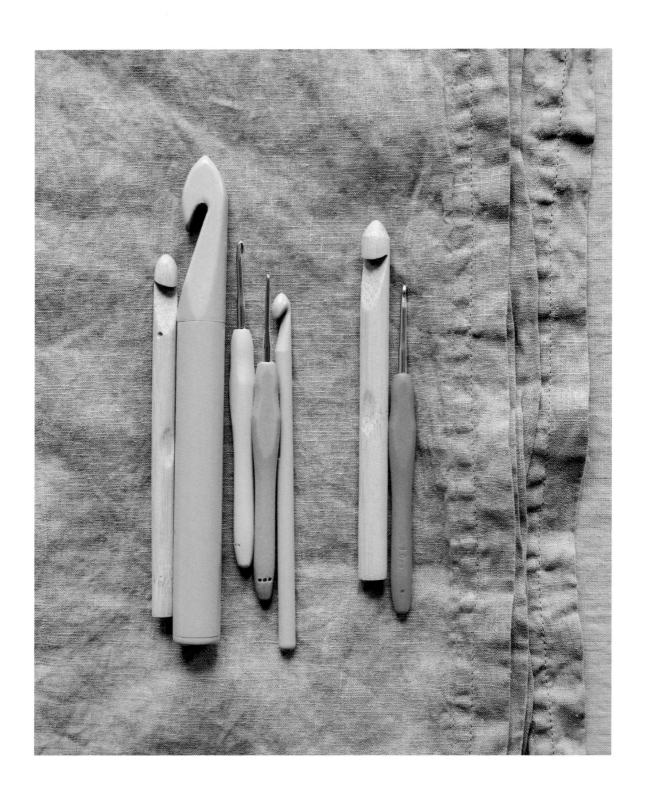

YARNS, HOOKS AND EQUIPMENT

For me, the satisfaction of pulling each loop through another is just as important within the process as the finished piece. However, buying yarn and spending hour after hour creating each stitch is an investment and you will want that investment to end with something you will love. For this reason you will want to choose yarns that you really like, that are fit for purpose and will suit the project you've spent so a many hours crocheting.

Choosing a yarn for your project is often the best bit! Not only is it fun—because who doesn't love standing in front of a rainbow wall of yarn at your local yarn store! But also because the fiber you decide on for your project will massively affect the end result. If you're looking for something soft, draped and subtle, a nice cotton, linen or something containing silk would work really well. However, if your project needs something hardwearing, robust but luxurious, choose a wool, merino or fluffy mohair to get the glowing halo on your crochet. The same goes when choosing the weight of yarn to crochet with; a thinner yarn such as a sportweight (4ply) or light worsted (DK) will usually create a softer handle. Worsted (aran) or bulky (chunky) weight yarns make great oversized sweaters and accessories because they are thicker and can create a stiffer fabric.

Finding a good collection of hooks is something I spent lots of time researching. The material of your hook can massively affect your tension. Bamboo and wood tend to create a looser fabric compared to plastic or metal—as I mentioned in Swatching (see page 11), always make a gauge (tension) swatch before beginning a project and adjust your hook size accordingly. If you are finding this problematic, it's more important to match the stitch gauge (or get it as close as you can) than the row gauge. Personally, I like a hook with a silicone handle; I find they are most comfortable to work with and I love how they come in all different fun and funky colors.

There are a few other handy things to have in your crochet kit! A pair of scissors is a must, along with a ruler (if you can get a clear one with a grid, this is great for measuring gauge swatches). You will also need a tape measure, stitch markers (or use yarn and make little slip knots), a large-eyed sewing needle and a notebook and pen to jot down any notes or amendments throughout your project.

ABBREVIATIONS

alt	alternate
beg	begin(ning)
BLO	back loop only
BPdc	(back post double crochet) work dc stitch around back post of st from row below
BPtr	(back post treble) work tr stitch around back post of st from row below
ch	chain
ch-sp	chain space
cm	centimeters
cont	continue
dc	double crochet
dc2tog	double crochet 2 sts together
FLO	front loop only
foll	follow(s)ing
FPdc	(front post double crochet) work dc stitch around front post of st from row below

FPtr	(front post treble) work tr stitch around front post of st from row below
htr	half treble
htr2tog	half treble 2 sts together
opp	opposite
PM	place marker
rep	repeat
RS	right side
sl st	slip stitch
SM	slip marker
sp	space
st(s)	stitch(es)
tr	treble
tr2tog	treble 2 sts together
WS	wrong side
yo	yarn over
( )	work all stitches within brackets into the stitch or space stated
*	rep sequence from * the number of times stated
[ ]	rep sequence in square brackets the number of times stated

Crochet terms

All the patterns in this book are written using US crochet terms. See the table below for equivalent UK terms.

US term	UK term
single crochet (sc)	double crochet (dc)
half double crochet (hdc)	half treble crochet (htr)
double crochet (dc)	treble crochet (tr)
yarn over (yo)	yarn round hook (yrh)

Accessories

This section is all about the staples. Along with some great techniques to practice, such as working in the round or perfecting a sock heel, I wanted it to be a collection of capsule pieces for your wardrobe. Within this section you will also learn how to crochet a ribbed hat, create a raffia backpack, work a cotton rope clutch, and create your very own super chunky scarf with a pretty and effective herringbone stitch.

My favorite project here is Rebel (page 53), because who doesn't love a classic ribbed hat? It's a great evening project, it crochets up pretty quickly and I find something so satisfying in making the same project but in many different colorways and stripes.

Along with working with raffia in Dottie (page 35) to make a cool backpack, this section also covers using an array of different weights and yarn fibers. It would be fun to mix them up a little and maybe create a cotton backpack or a raffia clutch. The possibilities within this section are endless—no matter how many times you've made each project, there will always be another new idea to try!

MAE COTTON ROPE CLUTCH

Page 29

**DOTTIE
RAFFIA
BACKPACK**

Page 35

PEARL HERRINGBONE SCARF

Page 47

REBEL RIBBED HAT

Page 53

MAE

Cotton Rope Clutch

If you're looking for a fun and funky weekend project, then look no further. This bag is a great addition to your wardrobe and can easily be adapted by changing the inner color from black to one that will match your favorite go-to outfit!

Technique

Working in rounds

Size

One size

Width	10 ⅝ in
	27 cm
Height	10 ⅝ in
	27 cm

Yarn

Super bulky (super chunky)
Sample made in:
Bobbiny Braided Cord 5 mm
 (100% recycled cotton,
 109 yd/100 m per 17½ oz/
 500 g skein/hank)
1 skein of Golden Natural (A)
1 skein of Black (B)

Hook and Equipment

US 15 (10 mm) crochet hook
Stitch marker
Yarn needle

Gauge (Tension)

6.5 sts x 8 rounds to 4 x 4 in
(10 x 10 cm) working single
crochet, using US 15 (10 mm)
crochet hook or size to obtain
stated gauge.

MAKE

Bag Face (make 2)

Using A, ch 3, sl st into first ch to create ring.
Round 1: 5 sc into ring, Work in a continuous spiral.
Round 2: 2 sc in every st. *10 sts*
Round 3: *1 sc in next st, 2 sc in next st; rep from * to end. *15 sts*
Round 4: *1 sc in next 2 sts, 2 sc in next st; rep from * to end. *20 sts*
Round 5: *1 sc in next 3 sts, 2 sc in next st; rep from * to end. *25 sts*
Round 6: *1 sc in next 4 sts, 2 sc in next st; rep from * to end, turn. *30 sts*
Beg working in rows.
Next row: Ch 1, [2 sc in next st, 1 sc in next 5 sts] 4 times, 2 sc in last st, turn. *30 sts*
Next row: Ch 1, [2 sc in next st, 1 sc in next 6 sts] 4 times, 2 sc in next st, 1 sc in last st, turn. *35 sts*
Ch 5, 1 sc in first st after gap/handle, [2 sc in next st, 1 sc in next 7 sts] 4 times, 2 sc in next st, 1 sc in next st, 1 sc in each of 5 ch, 1 sc in first st after gap.
Beg work in rounds again, PM to indicate beg/end of each round.
Next round: [2 sc in next st, 1 sc in next 8 sts] 5 times, sl st in first sc of round to join.
Fasten off.

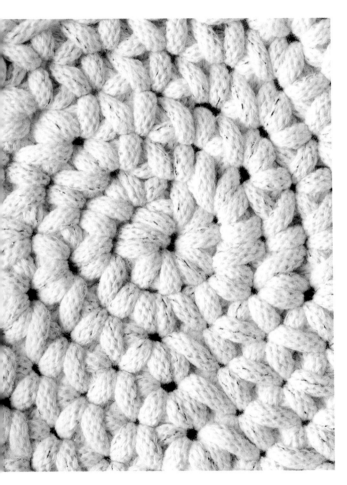

Side panel

Using B, ch 5.

Row 1: 1 sc in second ch from hook (skipped ch does not count as a st), 1 sc in next 3 ch, turn. *4 sts*

Row 2: Ch 1 (does not count as a st), 1 sc in every st, turn.

Rep Row 2 until work measures approx. 18½in (47 cm), ending with RS facing. Fasten off.

Making up

Using A and a single crochet seam, join the side panel to the first bag face then repeat to add the second bag face to the other side of side panel, leaving the top of bag open across the handles.

Weave in any loose ends. Press/block garment referring to ball band for instructions.

DOTTIE

Raffia Backpack

One of my favorite things about summer is getting out my raffia bag and I love working with this Ra-Ra raffia yarn because it comes in some lovely colors. You can make this for yourself or it makes a great gift—and the best thing about it is that you can customize the strap length to fit with the wearer. The backpack would also look great with a bright colour trim; think natural raffia and pastel linen!

Technique

Crocheting with raffia

Size

One size

Width	8¼ in 21 cm
Height	8¾ in 22 cm
Strap Length	24½ in 62 cm

Yarn

Light worsted (DK)
Sample made in:
Wool and the Gang Ra-Ra Raffia
   (100% raffia, 273 yd/250 m per
   3½ oz/100 g cone)
1 cone of Coal Black (A)
Rico Essentials Organic Cotton Aran
   (100% cotton, 98 yd/90 m per
   1¾ oz/50 g ball)
1 ball of White shade 1 (B)

Extras

1 small clear button

Hook and equipment

US 6 (4 mm) crochet hook
Sewing needle and thread

Gauge (Tension)

12 sts x 14.5 rows to 4 x 4 in
(10 x 10 cm) working single crochet,
using US 6 (4 mm) crochet hook
or size to obtain stated gauge.
13 sts x 6 rows to 4 x 4 in (10 x 10 cm)
working double crochet, using US 6
(4 mm) crochet hook or size to obtain
stated gauge.

MAKE

Sides (make 2)

Using A, ch 15.
Row 1: 1 dc in third ch from hook (skipped ch do not count as a st), 1 dc in every ch to end, turn. *13 sts*
Row 2: Ch 3 (does not count as a st), 1 dc in every st, turn.
Rep Row 2 another 13 times more or until work measures 8¾ in (22 cm), ending with WS facing.
Fasten off.

Base

Using A, ch 15.
Row 1: 1 dc in third ch from hook (skipped ch do not count as a st), 1 dc in every ch to end, turn. *13 sts*
Row 2: Ch 3 (does not count as a st), 1 dc in every st, turn.
Rep Row 2 another 13 times more, ending with WS facing.
Fasten off.

Back/front (make 2)

Using A, ch 27.
Row 1: 1 sc in second ch from hook (skipped ch does not count as a st), 1 sc in every ch to end, turn. *26 sts*
Row 2: Ch 1 (does not count as a st), 1 sc in every st, turn.
Rep Row 2 until work measures approx. 8¾ in (22 cm), ending with RS facing.
Fasten off.

Flap

Using A, ch 16.

Row 1: 2 sc in second ch from hook (skipped ch does not count as a st), 1 sc in every st to last st, 2 sc in last st, turn. *17 sts*

Row 2: Ch 1 (does not count as a st throughout), 2 sc in first st, 1 sc in every st to last st, 2 sc in last st, turn. *19 sts*

Rep Row 2 to 23 sts.

Next row: Ch 1, 1 sc in every st, turn.

Next row: Ch 1, 2 sc in first st, 1 sc in every st to last st, 2 sc in last st, turn. *25 sts*

Next row: Ch 1, 1 sc in every st, turn.

Next row: Ch 1, 2 sc in first st, 1 sc in every st to last st, 2 sc in last st, turn. *27 sts*

Now work straight in sc only until flap measures approx. 5 in (12.5 cm), ending with RS facing.
Fasten off.

Using B, work 54 sc evenly around outside edge of flap.
Fasten off.

Handle straps

Using A, ch 6.

Row 1: 1 sc in second ch from hook (skipped ch does not count as a st), 1 sc in every ch to end, turn. *5 sts*

Row 2: Ch 1 (does not count as a st throughout), 1 sc in every st, turn.

Rep Row 2 until work measures approx. 55⅛ in (140 cm).
Fasten off.

Making up

With WS together and using A, join base, sides, front and back panels together with a single crochet seam to show on the RS of the backpack. With RS of back and flap facing and using A, join together along the fasten-off edge using a slip stitch seam. Sew the small clear button on the inside of the flap approx. 1 in (2.5 cm) up from the beginning chain of the flap and in the middle (you do not need a buttonhole as the button will easily go through the raffia).

Fold the handle/straps in half to make a loop for the handle. With the RS of the back facing and using A and running stitch, sew through all layers of the strap/handle to attach it to the center of the flap seam to create a handle 6¼ in (16 cm) long. Then join the other ends of the strap to the bottom of the backpack on either side.

Weave in any loose ends. Press/block garment referring to ball band for instructions.

NORMA

Socks

For me, working a sock heel is super satisfying. I love the way the increases and decreases sit each side of the foot and I find it fascinating how going from working in rounds to working straight then back to rounds again creates such a unique but elegant shape.

Technique

Turning a sock heel

Size

US size 7/8 (UK size 6/7, European size 39.5/41)

Width across foot	4 in
	10 cm
Heel to cuff height	5⅛ in
	13 cm
Foot length	9½ in
	24 cm

Note

The socks are one size, but the foot length is adjustable.

Yarn

Worsted (aran)
Sample made in:
Rico Essentials Merino Aran (100% virgin
  wool, 109 yd/100 m per 1¾ oz/50 g ball)
1 ball of Natural 060 (A)
2 balls of Saffron 066 (B)

Hook and Equipment

US 6 (4 mm) crochet hook
US 8 (5 mm) crochet hook
Stitch marker
Yarn needle

Gauge (Tension)

18 sts x 5 rows to 4 x 4 in (10 x 10 cm) working double crochet, using US 8 (5 mm) crochet hook or size to obtain stated gauge.

Pattern Tip

If you change the foot length remember you may need less or more yarn.

Image 1 (page 44) shows where to work to before decreasing your stitches.

The stitch markers in the images on page 44 demonstrate the placement of the htr sts already made.

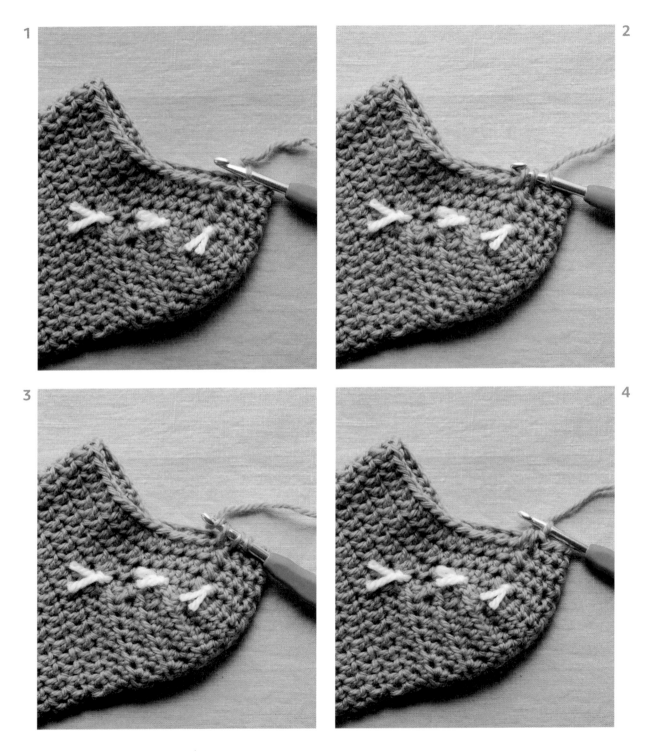

Htr2tog (half treble 2 sts together) (Insert hook into next stitch, pull up loop) twice (see image 2), yarn round hook (see image 3), pull yarn through all 3 sts on hook (see image 4).

MAKE

Socks (make 2)

Toe

Using US 8 (5 mm) hook and A, ch 3, sl st in third ch from hook to create ring.
Round 1: 12 dc in center of ring, PM to indicate beg/end of each round. Work in a continuous spiral.
Round 2: 2 dc in every st. *24 sts*
Round 3: *1 dc in next st, 2 dc in next st; rep from * to end. *36 sts*
Rounds 4, 5 and 6: 1 dc in every st. Change to B.
Next round: 1 dc in every st.
Rep last round 12 times more (work less or more length here if desired—work until approx. 1 in/2.5 cm less than final desired foot length).

Heel

Now work straight on next 18 sts only as foll:
Next row: 1 hdc in next 18 sts, turn.
Next row (WS): 1 hdc in next 18 sts, turn.
Next row: Hdc2tog over next 2 sts, 1 hdc in every st to last 2 sts, hdc2tog over last 2 sts. *16 sts*
Next row (WS): 1 hdc in next 18 sts, turn.
Rep last 2 rows 3 times more. *10 sts*
Evenly place 8 hdc down side of heel, work 18 hdc across front of foot, evenly place 8 hdc up side of heel and then work 10 hdc across back of heel. *44 sts*

Beg working in rounds again. PM to indicate beg/end of each round.
Next round: Hdc2tog over next 2 sts, 1 hdc in next 6 sts, 1 dc in next 18 sts, 1 hdc in next 6 sts, hdc2tog over next 2 sts, 1 hdc in next 10 sts. *42 sts*
Next round: Hdc2tog over next 2 sts, 1 hdc in next 5 sts, 1 dc in next 18 sts, 1 hdc in next 5 sts, hdc2tog over next 2 sts, 1 hdc in next 10 sts. *40 sts*
Cont decreasing as set in last 2 rows to 36 sts.
Next round: 1 dc in every st.
Work last round 6 times more or to desired sock length, ending last round as foll:
Next round: 1 dc in every st, join with a sl st into top of first dc at beg of round.

Cuff

Change to US 6 (4 mm) hook.
Next round: 1 dc in BLO of every st.
Next round: *1 FPdc in next st, 1 dc in next st; rep from * to end.
Rep last round once more.
Next round: 1 sc in every st to end, join with a sl st into top of first sc at beg of round. Fasten off.

Making up

Weave in any loose ends. Press/block socks referring to ball band for instructions.

PEARL

Herringbone Scarf

Once you've mastered this technique you will want to make everything in herringbone crochet. Working this satisfying stitch pattern in a chunky yarn will certainly have you hooked! This project is another classic piece, a super chunky scarf that you can wear all winter long.

Technique

Crochet herringbone

Size

One size

Width	9¾ in
	25 cm
Length	67 in
	170 cm

Yarn

Super bulky (super chunky)
Sample made in:
Rowan Big Wool (100% merino wool,
    87 yd/80 m per 3½ oz/100 g ball)
5 balls of Linen shade 048

Hook and Equipment

US 15 (10 mm) crochet hook
Yarn needle

Gauge (Tension)

11 sts x 7 rows to 4 x 4 in (10 x 10 cm)
working herringbone pattern, using
US 15 (10 mm) crochet hook or size to
obtain stated gauge.

Pattern Tip

Use the step images for the technique
alongside the written pattern to get
the herringbone stitch correct.

MAKE

Scarf

Ch 28.
Turn ch so WS is facing, working into second
ch from hook place hook into BLO with WS
of ch still facing (see image 1 on page 50),
work 1 sc in this ch, cont working 1 sc in each ch
to the end, turn. *27 sts*
Beg working herringbone pattern as foll:
Row 1 (RS): Ch 1 (does not count as a st
throughout), 1 sc in first st, *insert hook into
left leg of sc just worked and then into next st
(see image 4 on page 50), pull up loop (3 sts on
hook), yo (see image 5 on page 51) and draw
through all 3 sts (see image 6 on page 51); rep
from * to end, turn.
Row 2: Ch 1, 1 sc in first st, turn work so RS
is facing, insert hook from WS of work into
left leg of st just worked and next st (see
images 5 and 6 on page 51), pull up loop
(3 sts on hook), yo and draw through all 3 sts;
rep from * to end, turn.
These 2 rows set herringbone pattern, rep them
until scarf measures approx. 63½ in (161 cm),
ending with RS facing.
Fasten off.

Making up

Weave in any loose ends. Press/block garment
referring to ball band for instructions.

5

6

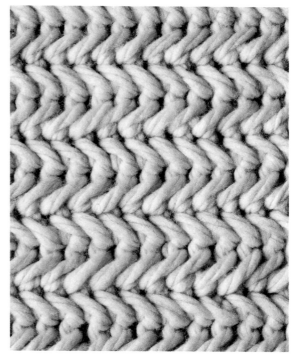

REBEL

Ribbed Hat

This is a staple accessory for the cooler months! You really can 'crochet it yourself' with this project and create different hats to match all your winter coats. Will you make yours in block color, stripes or in two-tone?

Technique

Classic beanie hat

Size

One size (stretched to fit average lady's head size)

Width	20½ in
	52 cm
Height	8¼ in
	21 cm

Yarn

Super bulky (super chunky)
Sample made in:
Erika Knight Maxi Wool
    (100% wool, 87 yd/80 m per
    3½ oz/100 g skein/hank)
One-color hat
1 ball of Iced Gem shade 216
Two-color hat
1 ball of Pretty shade 212 (A)
1 ball of Artisan shade 206 (B)

Hook and Equipment

US 15 (10 mm) crochet hook
Large-eyed sewing needle

Gauge (Tension)

8 sts x 5 rows to 4 x 4 in (10 x 10 cm)
working half double ribbing, using
US 15 (10 mm) crochet hook or size
to obtain stated gauge.

Pattern Tip

If you would like to adjust the height of
the hat, either remove chain stitches or
add more chain stitches to achieve the
desired height.

MAKE

One color hat

Ch 26.
Row 1: 1 hdc in second ch from hook (skipped
ch does not count as a st), 1 hdc in every ch
to end, turn. *25 sts*
Row 2: Ch 2 (does not count as a st), 1 hdc
in BLO of every st, turn.
Work Row 2 another 22 times more (24 rows
in total), until work measures approx. 19 in
(48 cm) stretched to fit average lady's head
circumference of 20½ in (52 cm), or work
to desired head circumference.
Join beg ch to last row of hat leaving
a long tail of yarn.
Fasten off.

Two color hat

Using A, ch 8, using B, ch 18.
Using B, work 1 hdc in second ch from hook
(skipped ch does not count as a st), 1 hdc in
next 16 ch, then work last 8 ch in A, turn. *25 sts*
Row 1: Using A, ch 2 (does not count as a st
throughout), 1 hdc in BLO of next 8 sts, using B,
1 hdc in BLO of next 17 sts, turn.
Row 2: Using B, ch 2, 1 hdc in BLO of next
17 sts, using A, 1 hdc in BLO of next 8 sts, turn.
Rep Rows 1 and 2 another 10 times more,
then work Row 1 again (24 rows in total). Work
should measure approx. 19 in (48 cm) stretched
to fit average lady's head circumference
of 20½ in (52 cm), or work to desired head
circumference.
Join beg ch to last row of hat leaving a long
tail of yarn.
Fasten off.

Making up

Join fasten off edge to beginning ch edge to make hat into a cylinder. Using a large-eyed sewing needle and running stitch, weave yarn end in and out of the fabric across right edge of hat (edge ending with B if doing two color) and pull tight to create crown of hat. Fasten off.

Weave in any loose ends. Press/block garment referring to ball band for instructions.

Sweaters

Sweaters are my secret love (hence why my first book, *KIY*, was all about them). I think they are the best blank canvas for stitch, texture, color or embroidery. This section is great for someone wanting to further their crochet skills and maybe try a garment for the first time. June (page 99) would be perfect—or if you're feeling a little more adventurous and want to try out a new stitch pattern, Avery (page 67) is the one for you.

My favorite project in this chapter is Imogen (page 75), named after my daughter because I made each granny square between, and sometimes during, feeds shortly after she was born. Along with the sentimental value of this project I just love a granny square project simply because it so easy. I like how transportable it can be—you make one anywhere and everywhere: watching TV, whilst catching up with a friend, or like me whilst feeding baby.

In this section you will perfect changing color, work loop stitch tassels, create the ultimate granny square, embellish with embroidery and finish off a garment with a classic ribbed neckband. Each sweater project is a basic boxy shape, a blank canvas for you to create and personalize to fit your own unique sense of style. So if you love a good sweater as much as I do, let's get started...

**AVERY
CROCHET RIBBED
EDGING SWEATER**

Page 67

**IMOGEN
GRANNY SQUARE
SWEATER VEST**

Page 73

GRACE TASSEL SWEATER

Page 83

MIA
TEXTURE
STRIPED
SWEATER

Page 91

JUNE
EMBROIDERED
SWEATER

Page 99

AVERY

Crochet Ribbed Edging Sweater

Mustard is one of my favorite colors, I think it goes well with anything and can be worn all year round. What better way to celebrate mustard than to frame it with black and white stripes? To me the perfect garment is one with all those final details and there's no better way to finish off a neckband than with classic ribbing. This project shows you how to work a faux crochet ribbing so you can get that perfect finish on your project.

Technique

Crochet ribbing

Size

	Small	Medium	Large	XL	XXL	XXXL	
To fit	32–34	36–38	40–42	44–46	48–50	52–54	in
	81–86	91–96	101–106	112–117	122–127	132–137	cm
Actual	41¾	45¼	48½	52	55½	59	in
	106	115	123	132	141	150	cm
Length	20½	21¼	21¼	22	22¾	23⅝	in
	52	54	54	56	58	60	cm
Sleeve length	17	17¾	18½	18½	19¼	19¼	in
	43	45	47	47	49	49	cm

* Model is wearing a size small.

Yarn

Light worsted (DK)
Sample made in:
Rico Essentials Merino DK (100% merino wool,
   131 yd/120 m per 1¾ oz/50 g ball)
8 (**9**, 9, **10**, 11, **12**) balls of Natural shade 60 (A)
3 (**4**, 4, **5**, 6, **6**) balls of Black shade 90 (B)
7 (**8**, 8, **9**, 10, **11**) balls of Mustard shade 70 (C)

Hook and Equipment

US 8 (5 mm) crochet hook
Yarn needle

Gauge (Tension)

9 reps of [1 sc, ch 1, 1 sc] x 16 rows to 4 x 4 in
(10 x 10 cm), using US 8 (5 mm) crochet hook
or size to obtain stated gauge.

Pattern Tips

1 When working the increases for the sleeves
work the first and last stitch of odd numbers,
where any skipped stitches would sit, as a single
crochet stitch.
2 Use mattress stitch instead of crocheting the
garment together to avoid the yarn showing on
the right side of the fabric.

MAKE

Back

Using A, ch 96 (**104**, 112, **120**, 128, **136**).
Row 1 (RS): 1 sc in second ch from hook (skipped ch does not count as a st), ch 1, 1 sc in same ch as first sc, *skip next ch, (1 sc, ch 1, 1 sc) in next ch; rep from * to end, turn. *48 (52, 56, 60, 64, 68) reps*
Row 2: (1 sc, ch 1, 1 sc) in first ch-sp, *(1 sc, ch 1, 1 sc) in next ch-sp; rep from * to end, turn.
Rep Row 2 six times more.
**Change to B.
Rep Row 2 twice more.
Change to C.
Rep Row 2 eight times more.
Change to B.
Rep Row 2 twice more.
Change to A.
Rep Row 2 eight times more.
The last 20 rows from ** form striped spider stitch pattern.
***Rep these 20 rows until work measures approx. 20 (**20¾**, 20¾, **21⅝**, 22½, **23¼**) in (51 (**53**, 53, **55**, 57, **59**) cm) from beg ch, ending with RS facing.

Shoulders

Keep stripe sequence set above correct throughout.
Next row: (1 sc, ch 1, 1 sc) in each of next 17 (**19**, 21, **22**, 24, **26**) ch-sps, turn.
Next row: Sc2tog over first two ch-sps, (1 sc, ch 1, 1 sc) in each of next 15 (**17**, 19, **20**, 22, **24**) ch-sps.
Fasten off.

Skip center 14 (**14**, 14, **16**, 16, **16**) ch-sps.
Re-join yarn to next 17 (**19**, 21, **22**, 24, **26**) ch-sps as foll:
Next row: (1 sc, ch 1, 1 sc) in each of next 17 (**19**, 21, **22**, 24, **26**) ch-sps, turn.
Next row: (1 sc, ch 1, 1 sc) in each of next 15 (**17**, 19, **20**, 22, **24**) ch-sps, sc2tog over last two ch-sps.
Fasten off.

Front

Work as for Back to ***.
Rep these 20 rows until work measures approx. 18⅛ (**18⅞**, 18⅞, **18⅞**, 19¾, **20½**) in (46 (**48**, 48, **48**, 50, **52**) cm) from beg ch, ending with RS facing.
Keeping stripe sequence as set correct throughout, work in spider stitch in next 21 (**23**, 25, **26**, 28, **30**) ch-sps, turn.

Front neck and shoulder

Next row (WS): Sc2tog over first two ch-sps, (1 sc, ch 1, 1 sc) in each of next 19 (**21**, 23, **24**, 26, **28**) ch-sps, turn.
Next row (RS): (1 sc, ch 1, 1 sc) in each of next 18 (**20**, 22, **23**, 25, **27**) ch-sps, sc2tog (first leg of sc2tog in last ch-sp and second in top of sc2tog from row below), turn.
Next row (WS): Sc2tog over sc2tog from row below and first ch-sp, (1 sc, ch 1, 1 sc) in each of next 16 (**18**, 20, **21**, 23, **25**) ch-sps, turn.
Next row (RS): (1 sc, ch 1, 1 sc) in each of next 15 (**17**, 19, **20**, 22, **24**) ch-sps, sc2tog (first leg of sc2tog in last ch-sp and second in top of sc2tog from row below), turn.

Now work straight in spider stitch keeping stripe sequence correct until work measures approx. 20½ (**21¼**, 21¼, **22**, 22¾, **23⅝**) in (52 (**54**, 54, **56**, 58, **60**) cm) from beg ch, ending with RS facing.
Fasten off.
Skip center 6 (**6**, 6, **8**, 8, **8**) ch-sps at center front neck and re-join yarn to shape right front neck and shoulder over last 21 (**23**, 25, **26**, 28, **30**) ch-sps as foll:
Keep stripe sequence as set correct throughout.
Next row (WS): Sc2tog over first two ch-sps, (1 sc, ch 1, 1 sc) in each of next 19 (**21**, 23, **24**, 26, **28**) ch-center sps, turn.
Next row (RS): (1 sc, ch 1, 1 sc) in each of next 18 (**20**, 22, **23**, 25, **27**) ch-sps, sc2tog (first leg of sc2tog in last ch-sp and second in top of sc2tog from row below), turn.
Next row (WS): Sc2tog over sc2tog from row below and first ch-sp, (1 sc, ch 1, 1 sc) in each of next 16 (**18**, 20, **21**, 23, **25**) ch-sps, turn.
Next row (RS): (1 sc, ch 1, 1 sc) in each of next 15 (**17**, 19, **20**, 22, **24**) ch-sps, sc2tog (first leg of sc2tog in last ch-sp and second in top of sc2tog from row below), turn.
Now work straight in spider stitch keeping stripe sequence correct until work measures approx. 20½ (**21¼**, 21¼, **22**, 22¾, **23⅝**) in (52 (**54**, 54, **56**, 58, **60**) cm) from beg ch, ending with RS facing.
Fasten off.

Sleeves (make 2)

Using A, ch 9.
Row 1: 1 hdc in second ch from hook (skipped ch does not count as a st), 1 hdc in every ch to end.
Row 2: Ch 1, 1 hdc in BLO of every st, turn.
Row 2 forms ribbing pattern.
Work in ribbing until cuff measures approx. 7⅛ (**7½**, 7⅞, **7⅞**, 8¼, **8¾**) in (18 (**19**, 20, **20**, 21, **22**) cm), ending with RS facing.
Now work down left-hand side of cuff to evenly place 27 (**29**, 31, **31**, 33, **35**) sts, turn.
Next row: 1 sc in first st, ch 1, 1 sc in same st as first sc, *skip next st, (1 sc, ch 1, 1 sc) in next st; rep from * to end, turn. *14 (**15**, 16, **16**, 17, **18**) reps*
Next row: (1 sc, ch 1, 1 sc) in first ch-sp, *(1 sc, ch 1, 1 sc) in next ch-sp; rep from * to end, turn.
Now work in 20 row striped sequence as set for Back in spider stitch **WHILST** increasing by adding an extra sc in first and last st at beg and end of next and then every 4th row, 14 (**17**, 18, **19**, 18, **20**) times more. *29 (**32**, 34, **35**, 35, **38**) reps*
Now work straight in striped sequence until sleeve measures approx. 17 (**17¾**, 18½, **18½**, 19¼, **19¼**) in (43 (**45**, 47, **47**, 49, **49**) cm), ending with RS facing.
Fasten off.

Making up

Join both shoulder seams. Join of last row of each sleeve to a shoulder seam and join each sleeve to garment body approx. 7⅛ (**7⅞**, 8¼, **8¾**, 8¾, **9½**) in (18 (**20**, 21, **22**, 22, **24**) cm) down each side of shoulder seam. Join each side and sleeve seam.

Neckband

Using A, with RS of Back neck facing and beg at right shoulder, evenly place 32 (**32**, 32, **34**, 34, **34**) sts across Back neck to left shoulder, then evenly place 16 (**16**, 16, **18**, 18, **18**) sts down left Front neck, 10 (**10**, 10, **12**, 12, **12**) sts at center Front neck and 16 (**16**, 16, **18**, 18, **18**) sts up right Front neck. *106 (**106**, 106, **116**, 116, **116**) sts*
Ch 9.
Row 1 (RS): 1 hdc in second ch from hook, 1 hdc in every ch to end, join to neck of garment with a sl st into first sc, turn. *8 sts*
Now work in ribbing as foll:
Next row: Ch 1, 1 hdc in BLO of every st to end, turn.
Next row: Ch 1, 1 hdc in BLO of every st to end working a sl st in every alt sc on neckband after last hdc is made, turn.
Rep last 2 rows until ribbing is complete and attached to every alt sc made for neckband. Fasten off.

Weave in any loose ends. Press/block garment referring to ball band for instructions.

IMOGEN

Granny Square Sweater Vest

This is probably my favorite garment from the book. I love the possibilities it brings: where shall I place each square? What color palette will I put together? How shall I join the squares together? What will I wear it with? And don't forget the possible future projects you can make when you've mastered the granny square technique.

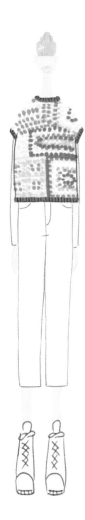

Technique

Granny squares

Size

One Size

Width under armholes	39⅜	in
	100	cm
Length	22	in
	56	cm

Note

Garment can be easily made bigger by making 2 more SQUARE F without neck shaping and adding them into each side seam. Remember you will need more of yarn C and D to do this and will need to add more dc sts when picking up for the armbands.

Yarn

Worsted (aran)
Sample made in:
Rico Essentials Merino Aran (100% virgin wool, 109 yd/100 m per 1¾ oz/50 g ball)
2 balls of Midnight Blue shade 039 (A)
2 balls of Natural shade 060 (B)
3 balls of Dusky Pink shade 014 (C)
2 balls of Red shade 008 (D)
1 ball of Sage shade 040 (E)

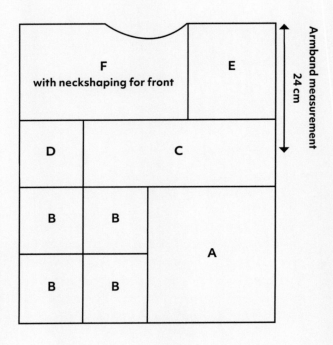

Hook and Equipment

US 8 (5 mm) crochet hook
Yarn needle

Gauge (Tension)

Square B measures 5½ x 5½ in (14 x 14 cm) using a US 8 (5 mm) crochet hook or size to obtain stated gauge.

MAKE

Square A (make 2)

Using C, ch 3, sl st in third ch from hook to create ring.

Round 1: Ch 3 (counts as first dc throughout), 2 dc in center of ring, *ch 2, 3 dc in center of ring; rep from * three times more, ch 2, join with a sl st into top of beg ch-3.
Fasten off C and change to B.

Round 2: Ch 3, 2 dc in corner ch-sp, (ch 2, 3 dc) in same ch-sp, *ch 1, (3 dc, ch 2, 3 dc) in next ch-sp; rep from * in each of next two ch-sps, ch 1, join with a sl st into top of beg ch-3.
Fasten off B and change to C.

Round 3: Ch 3, (2 dc, ch 2, 3 dc) in corner ch-sp, *(ch 1, 3 dc, ch 1) in next ch-sp, (3 dc, ch 2, 3 dc) in corner ch-sp; rep from * once more, (ch 1, 3 dc, ch 1) in next ch-sp, join with a sl st into top of beg ch-3.
Fasten off C and change to A.

Round 4: Ch 3, (2 dc, ch 2, 3 dc) in corner ch-sp, *(ch 1, 3 dc, ch 1) in next two ch-sps, (3 dc, ch 2, 3 dc) in corner ch-sp; rep from * once more, (ch 1, 3 dc, ch 1) in next two ch-sps, join with a sl st into top of beg ch-3.
Fasten off A and change to B.

Round 5: Ch 3, (2 dc, ch 2, 3 dc) in corner ch-sp, *(ch 1, 3 dc, ch 1) in next three ch-sps, (3 dc, ch 2, 3 dc) in corner ch-sp; rep from * once more, (ch 1, 3 dc, ch 1) in next three ch-sps, join with a sl st into top of beg ch-3.
Now cont as set above working (3 dc, ch 2, 3 dc) in each corner ch-sp and (ch 1, 3 dc, ch 1) in each ch-sp between each corner and working striped sequence as foll:

Round 6: Work in D.
Round 7: Work in E.
Round 8: Work in B.
Round 9: Work in C.
Round 10: Work in D.
Round 11: Work in A.
Fasten off.

Square B (make 8)

Work as set for Square A, beg with B and working striped sequence as foll:

Round 1: Work in B.
Round 2: Work in C.
Round 3: Work in D.
Round 4: Work in C.
Round 5: Work in E.
Round 6: Work in C.
Fasten off.

Square C (make 2)

Using E, ch 36.
Round 1: 2 dc in third ch from hook, ch 2, 3 dc in same ch, *miss 2 ch, 3 dc in next ch; rep from * to last 3 ch, miss 2 ch, (3 dc, ch 2, 3 dc, ch 2, 3 dc) in last ch, turn work upside down to work back along opp side of ch, *miss 2 ch, 3 dc in next ch; rep from * to end working last 3 dc in first of beg ch, ch 2, join with a sl st into first dc made.
Fasten off E and change to A.

Round 2: Ch 3 (counts as first dc throughout), (2 dc, ch 2, 3 dc) in corner ch-sp, (ch 1, 3 dc, ch 1) in each of next 11 ch-sps, (3 dc, ch 2, 3 dc) in corner ch-sp, ch 1, (3 dc, ch 2, 3 dc) in corner ch-sp, (ch 1, 3 dc, ch 1) in each of next 11 ch-sps, (3 dc, ch 2, 3 dc) in corner ch-sp, ch 1, join with a sl st into top of beg ch-3.
Fasten off and change to D.

Round 3: Ch 3, (2 dc, ch 2, 3 dc) in corner ch-sp, (ch 1, 3 dc, ch 1) in each of next 12 ch-sps, (3 dc,

ch 2, 3 dc) in corner ch-sp, ch 1, 3 dc in next ch-sp, ch 1, (3 dc, ch 2, 3 dc) in corner ch-sp, (ch 1, 3 dc, ch 1) in each of next 12 ch-sps, (3 dc, ch 2, 3 dc) in corner ch-sp, ch 1, 3 dc in next ch-sp, ch 1, join with a sl st into top of beg ch-3. Now cont as set above working (3 dc, ch 2, 3 dc) in each corner ch-sp and (ch 1, 3 dc, ch 1) in each ch-sp between each corners working striped sequence as foll:
Round 4: Work in C.
Round 5: Work in B.
Round 6: Work in A.
Fasten off.

Square D (make 2)

Work as set for Square A, beg with C and working striped sequence as foll:
Round 1: Work in C.
Round 2: Work in B.
Round 3: Work in C.
Round 4: Work in B.
Round 5: Work in C.
Round 6: Work in B.
Fasten off.

Square E (make 2)

Work as set for Square A, beg with C and working striped sequence as foll:
Round 1: Work in C.
Round 2: Work in B.
Round 3: Work in A.
Round 4: Work in C.
Round 5: Work in B.
Round 6: Work in C.
Round 7: Work in E.
Fasten off.

Square F (without neck shaping)

Using D, ch 27.
Round 1: 2 dc in third ch from hook, ch 2, 3 dc in same ch, *miss 2 ch, 3 dc in next ch; rep from * to last 3 ch, miss 2 ch, (3 dc, ch 2, ch 2, 3 dc) in last ch, turn work upside down to work back along opp side of ch, *miss 2 ch, 3 dc in next ch; rep from * to end working last 3 dc in first of beg ch, ch 2, join with a sl st into first dc made.
Fasten off D and change to C.
Round 2: Ch 3 (counts as first dc throughout), (2 dc, ch 2, 3 dc) in corner ch-sp, (ch 1, 3 dc, ch 1) in each of next eight ch-sps, ch 1, (3 dc, ch 2, 3 dc) in corner ch-sp, ch 1, (3 dc, ch 2, 3 dc) in corner ch-sp, (ch 1, 3 dc, ch 1) in each of next eight ch-sps, ch 1, (3 dc, ch 2, 3 dc) in corner ch-sp, ch 1, join with a sl st into top of beg ch-3.
Fasten off C and change to D.
Round 3: Ch 3, (2 dc, ch 2, 3 dc) in corner ch-sp, (ch 1, 3 dc, ch 1) in each of next nine ch-sps, ch 1, (3 dc, ch2, 3 dc) in corner ch-sp, ch 1, 3 dc in next ch-sp, ch 1, (3 dc, ch 2, 3 dc) in corner ch-sp, (ch 1, 3 dc, ch 1) in each of next nine ch-sps, ch 1, (3 dc, ch 2, 3 dc) in corner ch-sp, ch 1, 3 dc in next ch-sp, ch 1, join with a sl st into top of beg ch-3.
Now cont as set above working (3 dc, ch 2, 3 dc) in each corner ch-sp and (ch 1, 3 dc, ch 1) in each ch-sp between each corners working striped sequence as foll:
Round 4: Work in C.
Round 5: Work in D. **
Round 6: Work in C.
Round 7: Work in D.
Fasten off.

Square F (with neck shaping)

Work as for Square F without neck shaping to **.
Change to C.
With RS facing, miss top right corner ch-sp and next 5 ch-sps and work in sixth ch-sp as foll:
Round 6: Ch 3 (counts as first dc throughout) in sixth ch-sp, (3 dc, ch 1) in each of next six ch-sps, (3 dc, ch 2, 3 dc) in corner ch-sp, (ch 1, 3 dc, ch 1) in each of next four ch-sps, (3 dc, ch 2, 3 dc) in corner ch-sp, (ch 1, 3 dc, ch 1) in each of next 12 ch-sps, (3 dc, ch 2, 3 dc) in corner ch-sp, (ch 1, 3 dc, ch 1) in each of next four ch-sps, (3 dc, ch 2, 1 dc) in corner ch-sp.
Fasten off C.
Round 7: Re-join D to ch-3-sp made at beg of last round by working ch 3 (counts as 1 dc) in that ch-3-sp, (ch 1, 3 dc, ch 1) in each of next six ch-sps, (3 dc, ch 2, 3 dc) in corner ch-sp, (ch 1, 3 dc, ch 1) in each of next 5 ch-sps, (3 dc, ch 2, 3 dc) in corner ch-sp, (ch 1, 3 dc, ch 1) in each of next 13 ch-sps, (3 dc, ch 2, 3 dc) in corner ch-sp, (ch 1, 3 dc, ch 1) in each of next five ch-sps, (3 dc, ch 2, 1 dc) in corner ch-sp.
Fasten off.

Making up

Press/block all squares referring to ball band for instructions.

Following layout set on schematic join squares together to create sweater vest shape using a slip stitch seam or preferred sewing method, then join the shoulders and side seams leaving 9½ in (24 cm) open down each side of the shoulder seam for armholes.

Neckband

Using A and beginning at right shoulder work 32 sc sts across back neck to left shoulder, now evenly place 34 sc across Front neck, join with a sl st into first sc made. 66 sts
Next round: Ch 3 (does not count as a st throughout), 1 dc in every st, join with a sl st into first dc made.
Next round: Ch 3, *1 dc in next st, 1 BPdc in next st; rep from * to end, join with a sl st into first dc made.
Work last round once more.
Fasten off.

Armbands

Using A, with front of garment facing and beg at right underarm of work, work 40 sc up to shoulder seam, evenly place 40 sc sts down back of armhole, join with a sl st into first sc made. *80 sts*
Next round: Ch 3 (does not count as a st throughout), 1 dc in every st, join with a sl st into first dc made.
Next round: Ch 3, *1 dc in next st, 1 BPdc in next st; rep from * to end, join with a sl st into first dc made.
Work last round once more.
Fasten off.
Repeat for left armband with back of garment facing, beg at left underarm.

Weave in any loose ends. Press/block garment referring to ball band for instructions.

GRACE

Tassel Sweater

Who doesn't love a tassel? I have an Auntie who would wear tassels on everything if she could! The triangular placement of these tassels across the chest is super flattering to wear and beginning with the center loop tassel means that it's really easy to get the placement symmetrical.

Technique

Loop stitch tassels

Size

	Small	Medium	Large	XL	XXL	XXXL	
To fit	32–34	36–38	40–42	44–46	48–50	52–54	in
	81–86	91–96	101–106	112–117	122–127	132–137	cm
Actual	40¼	42½	46½	49¼	53¼	56	in
	102	108	118	125	135	142	cm
Length	21¼	21¼	23⅝	23⅝	26	26	in
	54	54	60	60	66	66	cm
Sleeve length	17	17¾	18½	18½	19¼	19¼	in
	43	45	47	47	49	49	cm

* Model is wearing a size small.

Yarn

Light worsted (DK) with 2 strands held together
Sample made in:
The Fibre Co. Arranmore Light (80% merino wool, 10% silk, 10% cashmere, 328 yd/ 300 m per 3½ oz/100 g skein/hank)
5 (**6**, 7, **7**, 8, **9**) skeins of St Claire

Hook and Equipment

US 11 (8 mm) crochet hook
Yarn needle

Gauge (Tension)

12 sts x 10 rows to 4 x 4 in (10 x 10 cm) working double and single crochet stripes with two strands of yarn held together, using US 11 (8 mm) crochet hook or size to obtain stated gauge.

Special Abbreviations

loop sc (loop single crochet): insert hook into st (see image 1, page 87), create length of loop with your finger (approx. 1¼ in/3 cm long) at front of work (RS of fabric)(see image 2, page 87), yo, pull up loop (loop made on RS of work).

loop dc (loop double crochet): yo, insert hook into st (see image 1, page 87), pull up loop, create length of loop with your finger (approx. 1¼ in/3 cm long) at back of work (RS of fabric) (see image 2, page 87), yo, pull up loop (loop made on RS of work)(see image 3, page 87).

MAKE

Front

Using 2 strands of yarn held together, ch 63 (**67**, 73, **77**, 83, **87**).

Row 1 (RS): 1 dc in third ch from hook (skipped ch do not count as a st), 1 dc in every ch to end. *61 (**65**, 71, **75**, 81, **85**) sts*

Row 2: Ch 1 (does not count as a st throughout), 1 sc in every st, turn.

Row 3: Ch 1, 1 sc in BLO of every st, turn.

Row 4: Ch 1, 1 sc in first st, *ch 1, skip next st, 1 sc in next st; rep from * to end, turn.

Row 5: Ch 1, 1 sc in first st, *1 sc in ch-1-sp, 1 sc in next st; rep from * to end, turn.

Row 6: Ch 1, 1 sc in every st, turn.

Row 7: Ch 2, 1 dc in BLO of every st, turn.

Rows 2–7 form dc and sc stripe pattern.

Repeat these six rows 2 (**2**, 3, **3**, 4, **4**) times more and then work Rows 2–6 again, ending with RS facing for next row.

Cont dc and sc stripe sequence as set above whilst placing tassels as foll:

Next row (RS): Ch 2, 1 dc in BLO of next 30 (**32**, 35, **37**, 40, **42**) sts, loop dc in next st, 1 dc in BLO of next 30 (**32**, 35, **37**, 40, **42**) sts turn.

Next row: Ch 1, 1 sc in next 29 (**31**, 34, **36**, 39, **41**) sts, loop sc in next st, 1 sc in next st, loop sc in next st, 1 sc in next 29 (**31**, 34, **36**, 39, **41**) sts, turn.

Next row: Ch 1, dc and sc stripe in next 28 (**30**, 33, **35**, 38, **40**) sts, loop sc in next st, dc and sc stripe in next 3 sts, loop sc in next st, dc and sc stripe in next 28 (**30**, 33, **35**, 38, **40**) sts, turn.**

Cont as set above, keeping dc and sc stripe correct throughout **WHILST** placing a loop sc or loop dc on appropriate row moving out one st every row until work measures approx. 18⅞

(**18⅞**, 21¼, **21¼**, 23⅝, **23⅝**) in (48 (**48**, 54, **54**, 60, **60**) cm), ending on Row 6 and RS facing for next row. If loop sc lands where (ch1, skip next st) should be worked, always work as loop sc.

Front neck shaping

Work in dc and sc stripe pattern over next 25 (**27**, 29, **31**, 33, **35**) sts as foll:

Next row: Dc and sc stripe in next 23 (**25**, 27, **29**, 31, **33**) sts, dc2tog, turn. *24 (**26**, 28, **30**, 32, **34**) sts*

Next row (WS): Sc2tog, dc and sc stripe to end, turn. *23 (**25**, 27, **29**, 31, **33**) sts*

Next row: Dc and sc stripe to end, sc2tog, turn. *22 (**24**, 26, **28**, 30, **32**) sts*

Next row: Sc2tog, dc and sc stripe to end, turn. *21 (**23**, 25, **27**, 29, **31**) sts*

Work 2 rows straight in dc and sc stripe.

Fasten off.

Skip center 11 (**11**, 13, **13**, 15, **15**) sts from before first side of neck is worked and work on last 25 (**27**, 29, **31**, 33, **35**) sts as foll:

Next row: Dc2tog, dc and sc stripe in next 23 (**25**, 27, **29**, 31, **33**) sts, turn. *24 (**26**, 28, **30**, 32, **34**) sts*

Next row (WS): Dc and sc stripe to end, sc2tog, turn. *23 (**25**, 27, **29**, 31, **33**) sts*

Next row: Sc2tog, dc and sc stripe to end, turn. *22 (**24**, 26, **28**, 30, **32**) sts*

Next row: Dc and sc stripe to end, sc2tog, turn. *21 (**23**, 25, **27**, 29, **31**) sts*

Work 2 rows straight in dc and sc stripe.

Fasten off.

Back

Work as for Front to **.
Cont as set above, keeping dc and sc stripe correct throughout **WHILST** placing a loop sc or loop dc on appropriate row moving out one st every row until work measures approx. 20½ (**20½**, 22¾, **22¾**, 25¼, **25¼**) in (52 (**52**, 58, **58**, 64, **64**) cm), ending on Row 4 and RS facing for next row. If loop sc lands where (ch1, skip next st) should be worked, always work as loop sc.

Shoulder shaping

Next row (RS): Keep dc and sc stripe and loop placement correct over next 20 (**22**, 24, **26**, 28, **30**) sts, sc2tog, turn. *21 (**23**, 25, **27**, 29, **31**) sts*
Work 1 row in dc and sc stripe with loop placement.
Fasten off.
With RS facing work over last 22 (**24**, 26, **28**, 30, **32**) sts from before right shoulder shaping as foll:
Next row (RS): Sc2tog, keep dc and sc stripe and loop placement correct over next 20 (**22**, 24, **26**, 28, **30**) sts, turn. *21 (**23**, 25, **27**, 29, **31**) sts*
Work 1 row in dc and sc stripe with loop placement.
Fasten off.

Sleeves (make 2)

Using 2 strands of yarn held together, ch 23 (**23**, 25, **25**, 25, **27**).
Row 1 (RS): 1 dc in third ch from hook (skipped ch do not count as a st), 1 dc in every ch to end. *21 (**21**, 23, **23**, 23, **25**) sts*
Row 2: Ch 1 (does not count as a st throughout), 1 sc in every st, turn.
Row 3: Ch 1, 1 sc in BLO of every st, turn.
Row 4: Ch 1, 1 sc in first st, *ch 1, skip 1 st, 1 sc in next st; rep from * to end, turn. (20 (**20**, 21, **22**, 22, **23**) cm).
Keep dc and sc stripe as set for front correct **WHILST** increasing at each end by working 2 sts in first and last sts of next and then every 4th row to 41 (**41**, 43, **43**, 43, **45**, 45) sts.
Now work straight in dc and sc stripe until work measures approx. 16⅛ (**17**, 17¾, **17¾**, 18½, **18½**) in (41 (**43**, 45, **45**, 47, **47**) cm), ending with RS facing for next row.
Next row (RS): Ch 1, loop sc in every st, turn.
Next row: Ch 1, 1 sc in every st, turn.
Fasten off.

1

2

3

Making up

Join both shoulder seams. Join center of last row of each sleeve to shoulder seams and join each sleeve to garment body approx. 7⅞ (**7⅞**, 8¼, **8¾**, 8¾, **9**) in (20 (**20**, 21, **22**, 22, **23**) cm) down each side of shoulder seam. Join each side and sleeve seam.

Neckband

With 2 strands of yarn held together, RS of Back neck facing and beg at right shoulder, evenly place 21 (**21**, 23, **23**, 25, **25**) sc across Back neck to left shoulder, then evenly place 6 sc down left Front neck, 11 (**11**, 13, **13**, 15, **15**) sc at center Front neck and then 6 sc up right Front neck. *44 (**44**, 48, **48**, 52, **52**) sts*
Ch 5.
Row 1 (RS): 1 hdc in second ch from hook, 1 hdc in every ch to end, join to neck of garment with a sl st into first sc. turn. 4 sts
Now work in ribbing as foll:
Next row: Ch 1, 1 hdc in BLO of every st to end, turn.
Next row: Ch 1, 1 hdc in BLO of every st to end working a sl st in every alt sc on neckband after last hdc is made, turn.
Rep last 2 rows until ribbing is complete and attached to every alt sc made for neckband. Fasten off.

Weave in any loose ends. Press/block garment referring to ball band for instructions.

MIA

Texture Striped Sweater

The inspiration for this project is all about color and placement—working different crochet stitches with a specific placement and color. This is a project in which you can let your creativity go wild! The rule I follow is always to pick an odd number of colors in my palette and always choose two base colors—here I use white and navy.

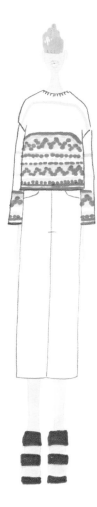

Technique

Color changing

Size

	Small	Medium	Large	XL	XXL	XXXL	
To fit	32–34	36–38	40–42	44–46	48–50	52–54	in
	81–86	91–96	101–106	112–117	122–127	132–137	cm
Actual	45¾	48½	53½	59	61¾	64½	in
	116	123	136	150	157	164	cm
Length	20½	21¼	22	22¾	23⅝	23⅝	in
	52	54	56	58	60	60	cm
Sleeve length	11¾	11¾	12½	13½	13½	14¼	in
	30	30	32	34	34	36	cm

* Model is wearing a size small.

Yarn

Light worsted (DK)
Sample made in:
Debbie Bliss Piper (50% cotton, 50% viscose, 219 yd/200 m per 3½ oz/100 g ball)
2 (**2**, 2, **3**, 3, **4**) balls of Dusk shade 6 (A)
4 (**4**, 5, **6**, 6, **7**) balls of Snow shade 1 (B)
2 (**2**, 3, **3**, 3, **4**) balls of Coral shade 17 (C)
2 (**2**, 3, **3**, 3, **4**) balls of Blush shade 11 (D)
1 (**1**, 1, **2**, 2, **2**) balls of Pool shade 10 (E)

Hook and Equipment

US 6 (4 mm) crochet hook
Yarn needle

Gauge (Tension)

17 sts x 8 rows to 4 x 4 in (10 x 10 cm) working double crochet, using US 6 (4 mm) crochet hook or size to obtain stated gauge.
18 sts x 17 rows to 4 x 4 in (10 x 10 cm) working striped pattern (multiples of 6+3), using US 6 (4 mm) hook or size to obtain stated gauge.

Special Abbreviation

MB (make bobble): [yo, insert hook into same stitch, yo, pull up loop, yo, pull through two loops] 4 times (5 sts on hook), yo and pull through all loops, ch 1 (does not count as a st) to secure bobble (bobble made).

Pattern Tips

1 Take care not to count the chain stitch at the top of the bobble as a stitch.
2 When beginning with a new color, introduce it on the last pull up loop of the last stitch on the row below to create a seamless color change.

To create a neat edge when changing the colour yarn you are working with stop at the last pull up loop of the last st on the row below (see image 1, page 94). Work the pull up loop with the new colour (see image 2, page 94) and then begin your new row (see image 3 and 4, page 94).

92

MAKE

Back

Using A, ch 106 (**112**, 124, **136**, 142, **148**).
Row 1 (RS): 1 sc in second ch from hook (skipped ch do not count as a st), 1 sc in every ch, turn. *105 (**111**, 123, **135**, 141, **147**) sts*
Row 2: Ch 1 (does not count as a st throughout), 1 sc in every st, turn.
Change to B.
Row 3: Ch 1, *1 sc in next st, ch 1, skip 1 st; rep from * to last st, 1 sc in last st, turn.
Row 4 (WS): Ch 1, *1 sc in next st, 1 sc in next ch-sp; rep from * to last st, 1 sc in last st, turn.
Change to A.
Row 5: Ch 3 (does not count as a st throughout), *skip 1 st, 2 dc in next st; rep from * to last st, 1 dc in last st, turn.
Row 6: Ch 1, 1 sc in every st, turn.
Change to C.
Row 7: Ch 1, 1 sc in every st, turn.
Row 8: Ch 1, *1 sc in next st, MB in next st, 1 sc in next st; rep from * to last st, 1 sc in last st, turn.
Change to D.
Row 9: Ch 2 (does not count as a st throughout), 1 dc in every st, turn.
Row 10: Ch 1, 1 sc in every st, turn.
Change to A.
Row 11: Ch 1, *1 sc in next st, ch 1, skip 1 st; rep from * to last st, 1 sc in last st, turn.
Change to B.
Row 12: Ch 3, *2 dc in every ch-sp; rep from * to last st, 1 dc in last st, turn.
Change to D.
Row 13: Ch 1, 1 sc in every st in D, turn.
Row 14: Ch 1, 1 sc in next st in D, *MB in next st in C, 1 sc in next 5 sts in D; rep from * to last 2 sts, MB in next st in C, 1 sc in last st in D, turn.

Row 15: Ch 1, 1 sc in every st in D, turn.
Row 16: Ch 1, 1 sc in next 2 sts in D, *MB in next st in C, 1 sc in next 3 sts in D, MB in next st in C, 1 sc in next st in D; rep from * to last st, 1 sc in last st in D, turn.
Row 17: Ch 1, 1 sc in every st in D, turn.
Row 18: Ch 1, 1 sc in next 4 sts in D, *MB in next st in C, 1 sc in next 5 sts in D; rep from * to last 5 sts, MB in next st in C, 1 sc in next 4 sts in D, turn.
Row 19: Ch 1, 1 sc in every st in D, turn.
Change to E.
Row 20: Ch 3, *skip 1 st, 2 dc in next st; rep from * to last st, 1 dc in last st, turn.
Change to A.
Rows 21 and 22: Ch 1, 1 sc in every st, turn.
Change to E.
Row 23: Ch 1, *skip 1 st, 2 dc in next st; rep from * to last st, 1 sc in last st, turn.
Change to C.
Row 24: Ch 1, *1 sc in next st, ch 1, skip 1 st; rep from * to last st, 1 sc in last st, turn.
Change to B.
Row 25: Ch 1, *1 sc in next st, 1 sc in ch-sp; rep from * to last st, 1 sc in last st, turn.
Row 26: Ch 3, *skip 1 st, 1 dc in next st, ch 1; rep from * to last 3 sts, skip 1, 1 dc in next 2 sts.
Row 27: Ch 1, 1 sc in next 2 sts, *1 sc in ch-sp, 1 sc in next st; rep from * ending with last sc in ch-3 from previous row, turn.
Row 28: Ch 1, 1 sc in every st, turn.
These 28 rows form texture striped pattern.
Rep these 28 rows once more beg with Row 1 in A as foll:
Row 1: Ch 1, 1 sc in every st, turn.
Now work Rows 2–28. Work should now measure approx. 12½ in (32 cm).
Continue in B.

Next row: Ch 3, 1 dc in every st, turn.
Rep last row once more.
Change to D.
Next row: Ch 3, *skip 1 st, 1 dc in next st, ch 1;
rep from * to last 3 sts, skip 1, 1 dc in next 2 sts.
Change to B.
Next row: Ch 3, 1 dc in next 2 sts, *1 dc in ch-sp,
1 dc in next st; rep from * ending with last dc
in ch-3 from previous row, turn.
Next row: Ch 3, 1 dc in every st, turn.
Rep last row 3 times more.
Change to E.
Next row: Ch 3, *2 dc in next st, skip 1 st; rep
from * to last st, 1 dc in last st, turn.
Change to B.
Next row: Ch 3, *1 dc in every st, turn.
Next row: Ch 3, 1 dc in every st, turn.**
Now work straight in dc only as set above
in B until work measures approx. 20½ (**21¼**,
22, **22¾**, 23⅝, **23⅝**) in (52 (**54**, 56, **58**, 60,
60) cm), ending with RS facing.
Fasten off.

Front

Work as for Back to **.
Cont in dc st as set above until work measures
approx. 18⅛ (**18⅞**, 19¾, **20½**, 21¼, **21¼**) in (46
(**48**, 50, **52**, 54, **54**) cm), ending with RS facing.
Now work left side of neck as foll:
Next row (RS): Ch 3 (does not count as a st
throughout), 1 dc in next 38 (**41**, 46, **52**, 55, **57**)
sts, dc2tog, turn. *39 (**42**, 47, **53**, 56, **58**) sts*
Next row: Ch 3, dc2tog, 1 dc in next 37 (**40**, 45,
51, 54, **56**) sts, turn. *38 (**39**, 46, **52**, 55, **57**) sts*
Next row: Ch 3, 1 dc in next 36 (**39**, 44, **50**, 53,
55) sts, dc2tog, turn. *37 (**40**, 45, **51**, 54, **56**) sts*

Next row: Ch 3, dc2tog, 1 dc in next 35 (**38**, 43,
49, 52, **54**) sts, turn. *36 (**39**, 44, **50**, 53, **55**) sts*
Next row: Ch 3, 1 dc in next 34 (**37**, 42, **48**, 51,
53) sts, dc2tog, turn. *35 (**38**, 43, **49**, 52, **54**) sts*
Now work straight in dc st until work measures
approx. 20½ (**21¼**, 22, **22¾**, 23⅝, **23⅝**) in (52
(**54**, 56, **58**, 60, **60**) cm), ending with RS facing.
Fasten off.
Re-join yarn to last 40 (**43**, 48, **54**, 57, **59**)
sts from before left side of neck was worked
skipping center 25 (**25**, 27, **27**, 27, **29**) sts as foll:
Next row (RS): Ch 3, dc2tog, 1 dc in next 38
(**41**, 46, **52**, 55, **57**) sts, turn. *39 (**42**, 47, **53**,
56, **58**) sts*
Next row: Ch 3, 1 dc in next 37 (**40**, 45, **51**, 54,
56) sts, dc2tog, turn. *38 (**39**, 46, **52**, 55, **57**) sts*
Next row: Ch 3, dc2tog, 1 dc in next 36 (**39**, 44,
50, 53, **55**) sts, turn. *37 (**40**, 45, **51**, 54, **56**) sts*
Next row: Ch 3, 1 dc in next 35 (**38**, 43, **49**, 52,
54) sts, dc2tog, turn. *36 (**39**, 44, **50**, 53, **55**) sts*
Next row: Ch 3, dc2tog, 1 sc in next 34 (**37**, 42,
48, 51, **53**) sts, turn. *35 (**38**, 43, **49**, 52, **54**) sts*
Now work straight in dc st until work measures
approx. 20½ (**21¼**, 22, **22¾**, 23⅝, **23⅝**) in (52
(**54**, 56, **58**, 60, **60**) cm), ending with RS facing.
Fasten off.

Sleeves (make 2)

Using A, ch 76 (**76**, 76, **82**, 82, **88**).
Row 1 (RS): 1 sc in second ch from hook
(skipped ch do not count as a st), 1 sc in every
ch, turn. *75 (**75**, 75, **81**, 81, **87**) sts*
Now work in texture stripe pattern as set
for back beg at Row 2 until all 28 rows are
completed.
Cont in B.

Next row: Ch 3 (does not count as a st throughout), 1 dc in every st, turn.
Rep last row once more.
Change to D.
Next row: Ch 3, *skip 1 st, 1 dc in next st, ch 1; rep from * to last 2 sts, ch 1, 1 dc in next 2 sts.
Change to B.
Next row: Ch 3, 1 dc in next 2 sts, *1 dc in ch-sp, 1 dc in next st; rep from * ending with last dc in ch-3 from previous row, turn.
Next row: Ch 3, 1 dc in every st, turn.
Rep last row 3 times more.
Change to E.
Next row: Ch 3, *2 dc in next st, skip 1 st; rep from * to last st, 1 dc in last st, turn.
Change to B.
Next row: Ch 3, *1 dc in next st, 1 dc in ch-sp; rep from * to last st, 1 dc in last st, turn.
Next row: Ch 3, 1 dc in every st, turn.
Now work straight in dc only as set in last row until work measures approx. 11¾ (**11¾**, 12⅝, **13⅜**, 13⅜, **14¼**) in (30 (**30**, 32, **34**, 34, **36**) cm), ending with RS facing.
Fasten off.

Making up

Join both shoulder seams. Join center of last row of each sleeve to shoulder seams and join each sleeve to garment body approx. 8¼ (**8¼**, 8¼, **8⅞**, 8⅞, **9½**) in (21 (**21**, 21, **22.5**, 22.5, **24**) cm) down each side of shoulder seam. Join each side and sleeve seam.

Neckband

With RS of back neck facing and beg at right shoulder, evenly place 34 (**34**, 34, **36**, 36, **38**) sc across back neck to left shoulder, then evenly place 11 sc down left front neck, 25 (**25**, 27, **27**, 27, **29**) sc at center front neck and then 10 sc up right front neck, sl st into first sc made to begin working in rounds. *80 (**80**, 82, **84**, 84, **88**) sts*
Round 1: Ch 3, 1 dc in every st to end.
Round 2: Ch 3, *1 FPdc in next st, 1 dc in next st; rep from to end.
Round 3: 1 sc in every st to end.
Fasten off.

Weave in any loose ends. Press/block garment referring to ball band for instructions.

JUNE

Embroidered Sweater

I named this sweater after my Nan, not just because she made this garment for the photography but because anything pretty, floral and lilac always reminds me of her—especially the lazy daisy stitch. The yoke is embellished with French knots, running and chain stitch as well as lazy daisies, which are all simple embroidery stitches that are great for beginners. When worked together they look more complex and are pretty effective, in my opinion!

Technique

Embroidery on crochet

Size

	Small	Medium	Large	XL	XXL	XXXL	
To fit	32–34	36–38	40–42	44–46	48–50	52–54	in
	81–86	91–96	101–106	112–117	122–127	132–137	cm
Actual	51¼	55⅛	59	63	67	70⅞	in
	130	140	150	160	170	180	cm
Length	20½	21¼	22	22¾	23⅝	23⅝	in
	52	54	56	58	60	60	cm
Sleeve length	17	17¾	18½	18½	19¼	19¼	in
	43	45	47	47	49	49	cm

* Model is wearing a size small.

Yarn

Light worsted (DK)
Sample made in:
Rowan Alpaca Soft DK (70% virgin wool, 30% alpaca, 136 yd/125 m per 1¾ oz/50 g ball)
14 (**15**, 16, **17**, 17, **18**) balls of Trench Coat shade 202
Other yarns for embroidery

Hook and Equipment

US 6 (4 mm) crochet hook
Yarn needle

Gauge (Tension)

16 sts x 17 rows to 4 x 4 in (10 x 10 cm) working single crochet, using US 6 (4 mm) crochet hook or size to obtain stated gauge.

Pattern Tip

For the embroidery you could use scraps from other projects you've made or yarns from your stash.

MAKE

Back

Ch 105 (**113**, 121, **129**, 137, **145**).

Row 1 (RS): 1 sc in second ch from hook (skipped ch does not count as a st), 1 sc in every ch to end. *104 (**112**, 120, **128**, 136, **144**) sts*

Row 2: Ch 1 (does not count as a st throughout), 1 sc in every st, turn.

Row 3: Ch 1, 1 sc in BLO of every st, turn.

Row 4 (WS): Ch 1, 1 sc in every st, turn.

Row 5: Ch 1, 1 sc in every st, turn.

Rows 2–5 form striped sc st pattern. **

Cont in striped sc st as set above until work measures approx. 19¾ (**20½**, 21¼, **22**, 22¾, **22¾**) in (50 (**52**, 54, **56**, 58, **58**) cm), ending with RS facing.

Next row (RS): Ch 1, 1 sc in next 37 (**41**, 43, **47**, 50, **53**) sts, sc2tog, turn. *38 (**42**, 44, **48**, 51, **54**) sts*

Now work straight in sc st until work measures approx. 20½ (**21¼**, 22, **22¾**, 23⅝, **23⅝**) in (52 (**54**, 56, **58**, 60, **60**) cm), ending with RS facing. Fasten off.

Re-join yarn to last 39 (**43**, 45, **49**, 52, **55**) sts from before right shoulder was worked, missing center 26 (**26**, 30, **30**, 32, **34**) sts as foll:

Next row (RS): Ch 1, sc2tog, 1 sc in next 37 (**41**, 43, **47**, 50, **53**) sts, turn. *38 (**42**, 44, **48**, 51, **54**) sts*

Now work straight in sc st until work measures approx. 20½ (**21¼**, 22, **22¾**, 23⅝, **23⅝**) in (52 (**54**, 56, **58**, 60, **60**) cm), ending with RS facing. Fasten off.

Front

Work as for Back to **.

Cont in sc st as set above until work measures approx. 17¼ (**18⅛**, 18⅞, **19¾**, 20½, **20½**) in (44 (**46**, 48, **50**, 52, **52**) cm), ending with RS facing. Now work left side of neck as foll:

Next row (RS): Ch 1, 1 sc in next 41 (**45**, 47, **51**, 54, **57**) sts, sc2tog, turn. *42 (**46**, 48, **52**, 55, **58**) sts*

Next row: Sc2tog, 1 sc in next 40 (**44**, 46, **50**, 53, **56**) sts, turn. *41 (**45**, 47, **51**, 54, **57**) sts*

Next row: Ch 1, 1 sc in next 39 (**43**, 45, **49**, 52, **55**) sts, sc2tog, turn. *40 (**44**, 46, **50**, 53, **56**) sts*

Next row: Sc2tog, 1 sc in next 38 (**42**, 44, **48**, 51, **54**) sts, turn. *39 (**43**, 45, **49**, 52, **55**) sts*

Next row: Ch 1, 1 sc in next 37 (**41**, 43, **47**, 50, **53**) sts, sc2tog, turn. *38 (**42**, 44, **48**, 51, **54**) sts*

Now work straight in sc st until work measures approx. 20½ (**21¼**, 22, **22¾**, 23⅝, **23⅝**) in (52 (**54**, 56, **58**, 60, **60**) cm), ending with RS facing. Fasten off.

Re-join yarn to last 42 (**46**, 48, **52**, 55, **58**) sts from before left side of neck was worked, missing center 18 (**18**, 20, **20**, 22, **22**) sts as foll:

Next row (RS): Sc2tog, 1 sc in next 41 (**45**, 47, **51**, 54, **57**) sts, turn. *42 (**46**, 48, **52**, 55, **58**) sts*

Next row: Ch 1, 1 sc in next 40 (**44**, 46, **50**, 53, **56**) sts, sc2tog, turn. *41 (**45**, 47, **51**, 54, **57**) sts*

Next row: Sc2tog, 1 sc in next 39 (**43**, 45, **49**, 52, **55**) sts, turn. *40 (**44**, 46, **50**, 53, **56**) sts*

Next row: Ch 1, 1 sc in next 38 (**42**, 44, **48**, 51, **54**) sts, sc2tog, turn. *39 (**43**, 45, **49**, 52, **55**) sts*

Next row: Sc2tog, 1 sc in next 37 (**41**, 43, **47**, 50, **53**) sts, turn. *38 (**42**, 44, **48**, 51, **54**) sts*
Now work straight in sc st until work measures approx. 20½ (**21¼**, 22, **22¾**, 23⅝, **23⅝**) in (52 (**54**, 56, **58**, 60, **60**) cm), ending with RS facing. Fasten off.

Sleeves (make 2)

Ch 33 (**33**, 34, **36**, 36, **38**).
Row 1 (RS): 1 sc in second ch from hook (missed ch does not count as a st), 1 sc in every ch, turn. *32 (**32**, 33, **35**, 35, **37**) sts*
Row 2: Ch 1 (does not count as a st throughout), 1 sc in every st, turn.
Row 3: Ch 1, 1 sc in every BLO of st, turn.
Row 4: Ch 1, 1 sc in every st, turn.
Row 4 forms sc st.
Cont in sc st as set above **WHILST** increasing at each end (by working 2 sc in first and last sts of row) of next and then every foll 4th row to 66 (**66**, 69, **71**, 71, **75**) sts.
Now work straight in sc stripe until work measures approx. 17 (**17¾**, 18½, **18½**, 19¼, **19¼**) in (43 (**45**, 47, **47**, 49, **49**) cm), ending with RS facing.
Fasten off.

Making up

Join both shoulder seams. Join center of last row of each sleeve to shoulder seams and join each sleeve to garment body approx. 7⅞ (**7⅞**, 8¼, **8¾**, 8¾, **9**) in (20 (**20**, 21, **22**, 22, **23**) cm) down each side of shoulder seam. Join each side and sleeve seam.

Neckband

With RS of Back neck facing and beg at right shoulder, evenly place 28 (**28**, 32, **32**, 34, **36**) sts across Back neck to left shoulder, then evenly place 10 sts down left Front neck, 18 (**18**, 22, **22**, 24, **26**) sts at center Front neck and then 10 sts up right Front neck. *66 (**66**, 74, **74**, 78, **82**) sts* Ch 7.
Row 1 (RS): 1 hdc in second ch from hook (missed ch does not count as a st), 1 hdc in every ch to end, join to neck of garment with a sl st into first sc, turn. *6 sts*
Now work in ribbing as foll:
Next row: Ch 1 (does not count as a st throughout), 1 hdc in BLO of every st to end, turn.
Next row: Ch 1, 1 hdc in BLO of every st to end, sl st into sc on neckband after last hdc is made, turn.
Rep last 2 rows until ribbing is complete and attached to every sc made for neckband as set. Fasten off.

Weave in any loose ends. Press/block garment referring to ball band for instructions.

Embroidery

Using a mixture of running stitch, chain stitch, lazy daisy stitch and French knots, get creative and work floral embroidery around the yoke and on the elbows of the garment. For placement you can use the photography as a guide or choose your own placement.

Lazy daisy stitch

Bring yarn up through the work where you want the centre of your flower to be, create a loop inserting needle back into the centre point and up through the loop at the length you want your daisy to be (see image 1, opposite), pull yarn but ensure petal is not pulled to tightly and insert needle into fabric at the other side of the yarn for petal (see image 2, opposite) and bring needle and yarn back up through the centre point (see image 3, opposite) and repeat process to create more petals (see image 4, opposite).

Cardigans

This is perhaps the most challenging section of the book because it features slightly more complicated techniques such as intarsia and tapestry crochet or inserting a pocket. But once you've mastered these techniques they will become quite easy and everything you make will include an invisible pocket—everyone loves a good practical pocket.

My favorite project from this section is Audrey (page 147); along with loving a chunky neutral cardigan in my wardrobe, I find the repetitive process of working bobbles so therapeutic and I love the billowing sleeves and the way they balloon at the cuffs.

In this section you will learn how to turn such classic prints, such as the leopard print and gingham, into crochet with a modern (yet customizable!) edge. In Kyra (page 121) you will perfect the technique for inserting a zipper into crochet and then in Ginny (page 139) how to add that invisible pocket, which brings us all such satisfaction.

WREN
STRIPED
POCKET
CARDIGAN

Page 113

KYRA ZIPPER CARDIGAN

Page 121

HAZEL
LEOPARD
CARDIGAN

Page 129

GINNY
GINGHAM
CARDIGAN

Page 139

AUDREY
BOBBLE AND
RIBBING
CARDIGAN

Page 147

WREN

Striped Pocket Cardigan

This is what I like to call the scrap yarn project of this book! You can use any fiber or any color for it, the more the merrier I say. If, like me, you're usually a little particular about your color placement, adding that alternate row of white really helps balance things out— but there's no reason why those stripes of white can't be different fibers. Let's help cut waste and use this project to make use of all those leftover and 'scrap' lengths of yarn.

Technique

Invisible pockets

Size

	Small	Medium	Large	XL	XXL	XXXL	
To fit	32–34	36–38	40–42	44–46	48–50	52–54	in
	81–86	91–96	101–106	112–117	122–127	132–137	cm
Actual	51¼	55⅛	59	63	67	70⅞	in
	130	140	150	160	170	180	cm
Length	22	22¾	23⅝	24½	25¼	26¾	in
	56	58	60	62	64	68	cm
Sleeve length	12⅝	12⅝	13⅜	13⅜	14¼	15	in
	32	32	34	34	36	38	cm

* Model is wearing a size small.

Yarn

Light worsted (DK)
Sample made in:
Paintbox Cotton DK (100% cotton, 137 yd/
   125 m per 1¾ oz/50 g ball)
8 (**9**, 10, **11**, 12, **13**) balls of Paper White
   shade 401 (A)
3 (**4**, 4, **4**, 5, **6**) balls of Dolphin Blue shade
   437 (B)
3 (**4**, 4, **5**, 5, **6**) balls of Raspberry Pink shade
   444 (E)
2 (**3**, 3, **4**, 4, **5**) balls of Rosy Pink shade 462 (G)
Rico Essentials Merino DK (100% merino wool,
   120 m/131 yd per 1¾ oz/50 g ball)
2 (**3**, 3, **4**, 4, **5**) balls of Mustard shade 70 (C)
Debbie Bliss Piper (50% cotton, 50% viscose,
   219 yd/200 m per 3½ oz/100 g ball)
2 (**3**, 3, **4**, 4, **5**) balls of Charcoal shade 19 (D)
Sublime Baby Cashmere Merino Silk DK (75%
   wool, 20% silk, 5% cashmere, 126 yd/116 m
   per 1¾ oz/50 g ball)
2 (**3**, 3, **4**, 4, **5**) balls of Fresh Lime shade 665 (F)

Hook and Equipment

US 6 (4 mm) crochet hook
Yarn needle

Gauge (Tension)

10 (sc and ch 1) sts x 10 rows to 4 x 4 in
(10 x 10 cm) working pattern, using US 6
(4 mm) crochet hook or size to obtain
stated gauge.

Pattern Tips

1 Use mattress stitch instead of crocheting
the garment together to avoid the yarn
showing on the right side of the fabric.
2 Just buy yarn A and use all different yarns
from your stash, or use up leftover yarns from
other projects!

MAKE

Back

Using A, ch 134 (**144**, 154, **164**, 174, **184**).
Row 1 (RS): 1 sc in fourth ch from hook (skipped ch do not count as a st), *ch 1, skip next ch, 1 sc in next ch; rep from * to end, turn. *131 (**141**, 151, **161**, 171, **181**) sts*
**Change to B.
Row 2: Ch 3 (does not count as a st throughout), *1 sc in ch-1-sp from row below, ch 1; rep from * to end, 1 sc in ch-3-sp from row below, turn.
Change to A and rep Row 2.
Change to C and rep Row 2.
Change to A and rep Row 2.
Change to D and rep Row 2.
Change to A and rep Row 2.
Change to E and rep Row 2.
Change to A and rep Row 2.
Change to F and rep Row 2.
Change to A and rep Row 2.
Change to G and rep Row 2.
Change to A and rep Row 2.
These 12 rows beg from ** form sc and ch 1 stripe pattern.***
Cont in stripe pattern until work measures approx. 22 (**22¾**, 23⅝, **24½**, 25¼, **26¾**) in 56 (**58**, 60, **62**, 64, **68**) cm), ending with a sc and ch 1 row in A.
Fasten off.

Pocket lining (make 2)

Using A, ch 31.
Row 1 (RS): 1 sc in fourth ch from hook (skipped ch do not count as a st), *ch 1, skip next ch, 1 sc in next ch; rep from * to end, turn. *28 sts*
Row 2: Ch 3 (does not count as a st throughout), *1 sc in ch-1-sp from row below, ch 1; rep from * to end, 1 sc in ch-3-sp from row below, turn.
Rep Row 2 until work measures approx. 5½ in (14 cm), ending with RS facing.
Fasten off.

Right and left fronts (make 2)

Using A, ch 74 (**81**, 84, **90**, 94, **100**) sts.
Row 1 (RS): 1 sc in fourth ch from hook (skipped ch do not count as a st), *ch 1, skip next ch, 1 sc in next ch; rep from * to end, turn. *71 (**77**, 81, **87**, 91, **97**) sts*
Now work in sc and ch 1 stripe pattern as set for Back from ** to *** until work measures approx. 7⅛ (**7⅛**, 7½, **7½**, 7⅞, **8¼**) in (18 (**18**, 19, **19**, 20, **21**) cm), ending with a sc and ch 1 row in A and WS facing.
Left front only
Now work in sc and ch 1 stripe pattern in next 11 (**12**, 13, **15**, 16, **17**) ch-sps, work next sc in next ch-sp of Left Front **AND** first ch-sp of Pocket Lining, then work sc and ch 1 in next 14 ch-sps on Pocket Lining only skipping 14 ch-sps on Left Front, and work sc and ch 1 in last 10 (**12**, 13, **14**, 15, **17**) ch-sps on Left Front, ch 1, 1 sc in ch-3-sp from row below, turn.

Right front only

Now work in sc and ch 1 stripe pattern in next 10 (**12**, 13, **14**, 15, **17**) ch-sps, work next sc in next ch-sp of Right Front **AND** first ch-sp of Pocket Lining, then work sc and ch 1 in next 14 ch-sps on Pocket Lining only skipping 14 ch-sps on Right Front, and work sc and ch 1 in last 11 (**12**, 13, **15**, 16, **17**) ch-sps on Left Front, ch 1, 1 sc in ch-3-sp from row below, turn.

Both fronts

Now cont straight in sc and ch 1 stripe pattern until work measures approx. 22 (**22¾**, 23⅝, **24½**, 25¼, **26¾**) in (56 (**58**, 60, **62**, 64, **68**) cm), ending with a sc and ch 1 row in A.
Fasten off.

Sleeves (make 2)

Using A, ch 84 (**84**, 86, **88**, 88, **90**) sts.
Row 1 (RS): 1 sc in fourth ch from hook (skipped ch do not count as a st), *ch 1, skip next ch, 1 sc in next ch; rep from * to end, turn. *81 (**81**, 83, **85**, 85, **87**) sts*
Now work in sc and ch 1 stripe pattern as set for Back from ** to *** until work measures approx. 12⅝ (**12⅝**, 13⅜, **13⅜**, 14¼, **15**) in (32 (**32**, 34, **34**, 36, **38**) cm), ending with a sc and ch 1 row in A and RS facing.
Fasten off.

Making up

Front bands

Using A and with RS facing, beg at garment hem of Right Front and evenly place 122 (**124**, 128, **130**, 132, **136**) sc to fasten off edge.
Next row: Ch 1 (does not count as a st), 1 sc in every st to end, turn.
Rep last row.
Fasten off.
Rep for Left Front with RS facing and beg at fasten-off edge.

To join Front to Back and create shoulder seams, join all fasten-off edges, overlapping Front by approx. 1 in (2.5 cm) at center to create Back neck point.
Join fasten-off row of each Sleeve to shoulder seams and join each sleeve to garment body approx. 7⅞ (**7⅞**, 8¼, **8¾**, 8¾, **9**) in (20 (**20**, 21, **22**, 22, **23**) cm) down each side of shoulder seam.
Join side and sleeve seams.

Weave in any loose ends. Press/block garment referring to ball band for instructions.

KYRA

Zipper Cardigan

Adding hardware, such as zippers and buttons, is another fantastic way to further your skills in crochet. There are so many great techniques for inserting a zipper but this one has to be my favorite. I love how you create a line of back stitch on the zipper tape, then attach it using crochet and it creates such a finished yet discreet look. Once you've mastered this technique you can add a zipper into any seam, cuff, hem or neckline that you want!

Technique

Placing a zipper

Size

	Small	Medium	Large	XL	XXL	XXXL	
To fit	32–34	36–38	40–42	44–46	48–50	52–54	in
	81–86	91–96	101–106	112–117	122–127	132–137	cm
Actual	47¼	51¼	55⅛	59	63	67	in
	120	130	140	150	160	170	cm
Length	20½	20½	21⅝	21⅝	22¾	23⅝	in
	52	52	55	55	58	60	cm
Sleeve length	17	17¾	18½	18½	19¼	19¼	in
	43	45	47	47	49	49	cm

* Model is wearing a size small.

Yarn

Light worsted (DK)
Sample made in:
Sirdar Snuggly Cashmere Merino Silk DK (75%
   wool, 20% silk, 5% cashmere, 126 yd/116 m
   per 1¾ oz/50 g ball)
14 (**14**, 15, **16**, 17, **18**) balls of Pied Piper shade
   305 (A)
1 (**1**, 1, **1**, 1, **2**) balls of Midnight shade 309 (B)
1 (**1**, 1, **1**, 2, **2**) balls of Goldilocks shade 311 (C)

Extras

5½ in (14 cm) zipper
Large eye pointed sewing needle

Hook and Equipment

US 6 (4 mm) crochet hook
Yarn needle
Large eye pointed sewing needle

Gauge (Tension)

17 sts x 22 rows to 4 x 4 in (10 x 10 cm) working
single crochet, using US 6 (4 mm) crochet hook
or size to obtain stated gauge.

Pattern Tip

A tip from my lovely knitter Gwen is if, like her,
you crochet left-handed you need to reverse
the shaping so that the zipper sits on the
correct seam.

MAKE

Back

Worked to armholes.
Using A, ch 100 (**108**, 118, **126**, 134, **142**).
Row 1 (RS): 1 sc in second ch from hook (skipped ch does not count as a st), 1 sc in every ch to end, turn. 99 (**107**, 117, **125**, 133, **141**) sts
Row 2: Ch 1 (does not count as a st throughout), 1 sc in every st to end, turn.
Rep Row 2 until work measures approx. 5½ in (14 cm), ending with WS facing.
Next row (WS): Ch 1, 1 sc in every st to end, ch 4, turn.
Next row: 1 sc in second ch from hook, 1 sc in next 2 ch, 1 sc in every st, turn. 102 (**110**, 120, **128**, 136, **144**) sts
Next row (WS): Ch 1, 1 sc in every st to end, turn.
Next row: Ch 1, 1 sc in every st to end, turn.
Cont in sc st as set in last row until work measures 11¾ (**11¾**, 12⅝, **12⅝**, 13⅜, **14¼**) in (30 (**30**, 32, **32**, 34, **36**) cm), ending with RS facing.
Next row: Ch 1, 1 sc in next 98 (**106**, 116, **124**, 132, **140**) sts, turn.
Next row: Ch 1, 1 sc in next 94 (**102**, 112, **120**, 128, **136**) sts, turn.
Fasten off (you will come back to working on these 94 (**102**, 112, **120**, 128, **136**) sts for Yoke.

Right front

Worked to armholes.
Using A, ch 48 (**52**, 58, **60**, 66, **70**).
Row 1 (RS): 1 sc in second ch from hook (skipped ch does not count as a st), 1 sc in every ch to end, turn. 47 (**51**, 57, **59**, 65, **69**) sts

Row 2: Ch 1 (does not count as a st throughout), 1 sc in every st to end, turn.
Rep Row 2 until work measures approx. 5½ in (14 cm), ending with RS facing.
Next row (RS): Ch 1, 1 sc in every st to end, ch 4, turn.
Next row: 1 sc in second ch from hook, 1 sc in next 2 ch, 1 sc in every st, turn. 50 (**54**, 60, **62**, 68, **72**) sts
Next row: Ch 1, 1 sc in every st to end, turn.
Cont in sc st as set in last row until work measures approx. 11¾ (**11¾**, 12⅝, **12⅝**, 13⅜, **14¼**) in (30 (**30**, 32, **32**, 34, **36**) cm), ending with RS facing.
Next row: Ch 1, 1 sc in next 46 (**50**, 56, **58**, 64, **68**) sts, turn.
Fasten off (you will come back to working on these 46 (**50**, 56, **58**, 64, **68**) sts for Yoke.

Left front

Using A, ch 51 (**55**, 61, **63**, 69, **73**).
Row 1 (RS): 1 sc in second ch from hook (skipped ch does not count as a st), 1 sc in every ch to end, turn. 50 (**54**, 60, **62**, 68, **72**) sts
Row 2: Ch 1 (does not count as a st throughout), 1 sc in every st to end, turn.
Rep Row 2 until work measures approx. 11¾ (**11¾**, 12⅝, **12⅝**, 13⅜, **14¼**) in (30 (**30**, 32, **32**, 34, **36**) cm), ending with WS facing.
Next row: Ch 1, 1 sc in next 46 (**50**, 56, **58**, 64, **68**) sts, turn.
Fasten off (you will come back to working on these 46 (**50**, 56, **58**, 64, **68**) sts for Yoke.

Sleeves (make 2)

Using A, ch 35 (**35**, 37, **39**, 39, **41**).
Row 1 (RS): 1 sc in second ch from hook (skipped ch does not count as a st), 1 sc in every ch to end, turn. *34 (**34**, 36, **38**, 38, **40**) reps*
Row 2: Ch 1 (does not count as a st throughout), 1 sc in every st to end, turn.
Row 2 forms sc stitch.
Cont in sc st **WHILST** increasing at each end by working 2 sts in first and last sts of next and then every 4th row to 68 (**68**, 72, **76**, 76, **78**) sts. Now work straight in sc until work measures approx. 16⅛ (**17**, 17¾, **17¾**, 18½, **18½**) in (41 (**43**, 45, **45**, 47, **47**) cm), ending with RS facing for next row.
Next row: Ch 1, 1 sc in next 64 (**64**, 68, **72**, 72, **74**) sts, turn.
Next row: Ch 1, 1 sc in next 60 (**60**, 64, **68**, 68, **70**) sts, turn.
Fasten off (you will come back to working on these 60 (**60**, 64, **68**, 68, **70**) sts for Yoke.

Yoke

Using A and with RS of Right Front facing, re-join yarn and work 46 (**50**, 56, **58**, 64, **68**) sc over sts left for yoke, PM, work 60 (**60**, 64, **68**, 68, **70**) sc for first Sleeve, PM, work 94 (**102**, 112, **120**, 128, **136**) sc for Back, PM, work 60 (**60**, 64, **68**, 68, **70**) sc for second Sleeve, PM and then work 46 (**50**, 56, **58**, 64, **68**) sc for Left Front, turn. *306 (**322**, 352, **372**, 392, **412**) sts*
Next row (WS): Ch 1 (does not count as a st throughout), 1 sc in every st to end, turn. Now work yoke and front neck decreases as foll:
Row 1: Ch 1 (does not count as a st throughout), 1 sc in next st, sc2tog over next 2 sts, 1 sc in next 40 (**44**, 50, **52**, 58, **62**) sc, sc2tog over next 2 sts, 1 sc in next st, SM, 1 sc in next st, sc2tog over next 2 sts, 1 sc in next 54 (**54**, 58, **62**, 62, **64**) sc, sc2tog over next 2 sts, 1 sc in next st, SM, 1 sc in next st, sc2tog over next 2 sts, 1 sc in next 88 (**96**, 106, **114**, 122, **130**) sc, sc2tog over next 2 sts, 1 sc in next st, SM, 1 sc in next st, sc2tog over next 2 sts, 1 sc in next 54 (**54**, 58, **62**, 62, **64**) sc, sc2tog over next 2 sts, 1 sc in next st, SM, 1 sc in next st, sc2tog over next 2 sts, 1 sc in next 40 (**44**, 50, **52**, 58, **62**) sc, sc2tog over next 2 sts, 1 sc in next st, turn. *296 (**312**, 342, **362**, 382, **402**) sts*
Row 2: Ch 1, 1 sc in every st to end, turn.
Row 3: Ch 1, 1 sc in next 41 (**45**, 51, **53**, 59, **63**) sc, sc2tog over next 2 sts, 1 sc in next st, SM, 1 sc in next st, sc2tog over next 2 sts, 1 sc in next 52 (**52**, 56, **60**, 60, **62**) sc, sc2tog over next 2 sts, 1 sc in next st, SM, 1 sc in next st, sc2tog over next 2 sts, 1 sc in next 86 (**94**, 104, **112**, 120, **128**) sc, sc2tog over next 2 sts, 1 sc in next st, SM, 1 sc in next st, sc2tog over next 2 sts, 1 sc in next 52 (**52**, 56, **60**, 60, **62**) sc, sc2tog over next 2 sts, 1 sc in next st, SM, 1 sc in next st, sc2tog over next 2 sts, 1 sc in next 41 (**45**, 51, **53**, 59, **63**) sc, 1 sc in next st, turn. *288 (**304**, 334, **354**, 374, **394**) sts*
Row 4: Ch 1, 1 sc in every st to end, turn.
These four rows form Yoke decreases every alt row, and front neck shaping every 4th row.
Cont as set a further 10 (**10**, 10, **10**, 11, **11**) times more, ending with RS facing. *108 (**124**, 154, **174**, 176, **196**) sts*
Medium, Large, XL, XXL and XXXL only
Note: For larger sizes adjust decreases accordingly to fit better across your shoulders

if more decreases are needed. Add more decreases in this row and work to either 108 or 118 sts to finish with correct stitch count for saddle. – (**124**, *154*, **174**, *176*, **196**) *sts*

Next row (RS): Ch 1, 1 sc in next – (**6**, 5, **3**, 16, **30**) sts, [sc2tog, 1 sc in next – (**5**, 2, **1**, 1, **0**) st/s] – (**16**, 36, **56**, 48, **68**) times, 1 sc in next – (**6**, 5, **3**, 16, **30**) sts. – (**108**, *118*, **118**, *128*, **128**) *sts*

All Sizes

*108 (**108**, 118, **118**, 128, **128**) sts*

Saddle

Re-join A at first marker.

Row 1: Ch 1, 1 sc in each st to second marker, turn.

Row 2: Ch 1, 1 sc in every st to end, turn.

Rep Row 2 twelve times more.

Fasten off.

Re-join A at third marker.

Re-join A at first marker.

Row 1: Ch 1, 1 sc in each st to second marker, turn.

Row 2: Ch 1, 1 sc in every st to end, turn.

Rep Row 2 twelve times more.

Fasten off.

Making up

Zipper band

Using B and with RS of Right Front facing, evenly place 24 sts along bottom 5½ in (14 cm) of edge down to garment hem.

Next row (WS): Ch 1 (does not count as a st throughout), 1 sc in every st, sl st into garment fabric to attach zipper band to Right Front, ch 1, turn.

Next row: Ch 1, 1 sc in every st, turn.

Next row (WS): Ch 1, 1 sc in every st, sl st into garment fabric to attach zipper band to Right Front, ch 1, turn.

Fasten off.

With B and RS of Back facing, evenly place 24 sts along bottom 5½ in (14 cm) of edge down to garment hem.

Next row (WS): Ch 1, 1 sc in every st, sl st into garment fabric to attach zipper band to Back ch 1, turn.

Next row: Ch 1, 1 sc in every st, turn.

Next row (WS): Ch 1, 1 sc in every st, sl st into garment fabric to attach zipper band to Back, ch 1, turn.

Fasten off.

Inserting zipper

Using a large eye sewing needle and B, and with zipper RS facing, create a line of back stitch along zipper tape with neat edge approx. ¼ in (5 mm) away from zipper teeth (see image 1, page 124). Remember your zipper needs to open from hem edge. Insert hook into first line of back stitch and into 1 stitch from fasten-off edge of zipper band (see image 2, page 124) and work a sl st (see image 3, page 124); rep inserting hook and working a sl st in next back stitch and next stitch from fasten-off edge of zipper band (see image 4, page 124) until this side of zipper is fully attached. Repeat for second side of zipper.

Join edge of each Saddle to last row of Yoke worked at both shoulders, then join Sleeve and side seams.

Front band
Using C and with RS of Right Front facing, evenly place 112 (**112**, 116, **116**, 118, **120**) sts to center Back neck point beg at hem of Right Front. Then evenly place another 112 (**112**, 116, **116**, 118, **120**) sts from center Back neck point to hem of Left Front. *224 (**224**, 232, **232**, 236, **240**) sts*

Next row: Ch 1 (does not count as a st throughout), 1 sc in every st, turn.
Rep last row six times more ending with RS facing.
Fasten off.

Weave in any loose ends. Press/block garment referring to ball band for instructions.

127

HAZEL

Leopard Cardigan

Leopard print is such a timeless classic, but there are so many ways to modernize it. Crochet intarsia creates a modern, summery version of this iconic pattern, which you can personalize with your favourite color and fiber. I've designed this garment in linen yarn to help create drape on a simple boxy style.

Technique

Leopard print tapestry intarsia

Size

	Small	Medium	Large	XL	XXL	XXXL	
To fit	32–34	36–38	40–42	44–46	48–50	52–54	in
	81–86	91–96	101–106	112–117	122–127	132–137	cm
Actual	47¼	51¼	55⅛	59	63	67	in
	120	130	140	150	160	170	cm
Length	24½	24½	26	26	27½	27½	in
	62	62	66	66	70	70	cm
Sleeve length	12⅝	12⅝	14¼	14¼	15¾	15¾	in
	32	32	36	36	40	40	cm

Model is wearing a size small.

Yarn

Light worsted (DK)
Sample made in:
Erika Knight Studio Linen DK (85% recycled rayon Linen, 15% premium linen, 131 yd/ 120 m per 1¾ oz/50 g skein/hank)
10 (**11**, 12, **13**, 15, **16**) skeins of Fatigue shade 403 (A)
4 (**5**, 6, **7**, 8, **9**) skeins of Kumo shade 411 (B)
2 (**3**, 4, **5**, 6, **7**) skeins of Bone shade 401 (C)

Hook and Equipment

US 6 (4 mm) crochet hook
Yarn needle

Gauge (Tension)

18 sts x 9 rows to 4 x 4 in (10 x 10 cm) working leopard instarsia pattern, using US 6 (4 mm) crochet hook or size to obtain stated gauge.

Pattern Tips

1 Lay inactive yarns over the hook at either back (on a RS row) or at the front (on a WS row) once the hook is inserted into the stitch (see Tapestry Intarsia Technique, page 137).
2 When working the intarsia crochet technique take care not to pull inactive yarns too tightly behind the work.

To work tapastry intarsia you need to change colour before you finish working the previous stitch (see image 1, page 132), you then pull up loop the the stitch before with the new colour (see image 2, page 132) and then begin working the next stitch (see image 3, page 132).

Inactive yarns will be trapped within treble sts (see image 4, page 132).

When working intarsia crochet technique take care not to pull inactive yarns too tightly behind work.

Key

- ■ **A** Fatigue
- ■ **B** Kumo
- □ **C** Bone

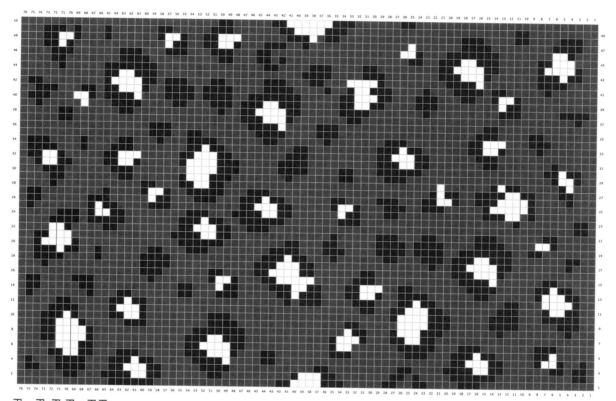

For size XXXL end here
For size XXL end here
For size XL end here
For size large end here
For size medium end here
For size small end here

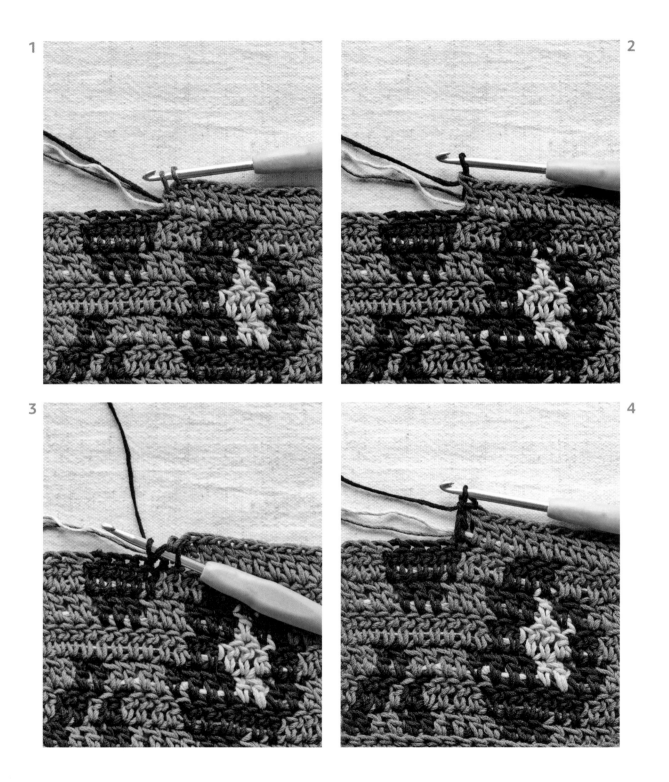

MAKE

Back

Work to armholes.
Using A, ch 221 (**233**, 253, **273**, 289, **305**).
Row 1 (RS): 1 sc in second ch from hook (skipped ch do not count as a st), 1 sc in every ch to end, turn. *220 (**232**, 252, **272**, 288, **304**) sts*
Row 2: Ch 1 (does not count as a st), 1 sc in every st to end, turn.
Now work from Chart, beg with Row 1 in BLO, introducing B and C using crochet intarsia technique (see images for tapestry intarsia technique) as stated, as foll:

Size Small only

Row 1 (RS): Ch 2 (does not count as a st throughout), [1 dc in A in BLO of next 5 sts, 1 dc in B in BLO of next 3 sts, 1 dc in A in BLO of next 4 sts, 1 dc in B in BLO of next 2 sts, 1 dc in A in BLO of next 2 sts, 1 dc in B in BLO of next 2 sts, 1 dc in A in BLO of next 5 sts, 1 dc in B in BLO of next 3 sts, 1 dc in C in BLO of next 4 sts, 1 dc in B in BLO of next 2 sts, 1 dc in A in BLO of next 16 sts, 1 dc in B in BLO of next 6 sts, 1 dc in A in BLO of last st] 4 times, turn.
Row 2: Ch 2, [1 dc in B in next 4 sts, 1 dc in C in next 2 sts, 1 dc in B in next 2 sts, 1 dc in A in next 6 sts, 1 dc in B in next 2 sts, 1 dc in A in next 9 sts, 1 dc in B next st, 1 dc in C in next 3 sts, 1 dc in B in next 2 sts, 1 dc in A in next 7 sts, 1 dc in B in next 2 sts, 1 dc in A in next st, 1 dc in B in next st, 1 dc in A in next 4 sts, 1 dc in B in next 6 sts, 1 dc in A in last 3 sts] 4 times, turn.

Medium, Large, XL, XXL and XXXL only

Work as set for size Small but begin and end working from chart at correct points for appropriate size.

All sizes

Rep Rows 1 and 2 from beg/end point as set on chart for appropriate size, but work Row 1 sts as normal and not in BLO, until work measures 15¾ (**15¾**, 16½, **16½**, 17¼, **17¼**) in (40 (**40**, 42, 42, 44, **44**) cm) from beg ch (once all 50 rows of chart are complete beg again at Row 1), ending with RS facing.
Split for Fronts and Back.

Right front

Keeping chart placement correct throughout, work over next 55 (**58**, 63, **68**, 72, **76**) sts, turn.
Cont on these 55 (**58**, 63, **68**, 72, **76**) sts only until work measures approx. 22 (**22**, 23⅝, **23⅝**, 25¼, **25¼**) in (56 (**56**, 60, 60, 64, **64**) cm), ending with RS facing.
Next row (RS): Ch 2, work in leopard pattern over next 43 (**46**, 51, **56**, 60, **63**) sts, dc2tog twice, turn. *45 (**48**, 53, **58**, 62, **66**) sts*
Next row: Ch 2, dc2tog twice, work in leopard pattern over next 41 (**44**, 49, **54**, 58, **62**) sts, turn. *43 (**46**, 51, **56**, 60, **64**) sts*
Next row: Ch 2, work in leopard pattern over next 39 (**42**, 47, **52**, 56, **60**) sts, dc2tog twice, turn. *41 (**44**, 49, **54**, 58, **62**) sts*
Next row: Ch 2, dc2tog twice, work in leopard pattern over next 37 (**40**, 45, **50**, 54, **58**) sts, turn. *39 (**42**, 47, **52**, 56, **60**) sts*
Cont on these 39 (**42**, 47, **52**, 56, **60**) sts only, keeping leopard pattern correct until work measures approx. 24½ (**24½**, 26, **26**, 27½, **27½**) in (62 (**62**, 66, **66**, 70, **70**) cm), ending with RS facing.
Fasten off.

Back

Re-join yarn to next 110 (**116**, 126, **136**, 144, **152**) sts keeping leopard pattern correct and working from chart.

Cont on these 55 (**58**, 63, **68**, 72, **76**) sts only in leopard pattern until work measures approx. 24½ (**24½**, 26, **26**, 27½, **27½**) in (62 (**62**, 66, **66**, 70, **70**) cm), ending with RS facing.

Fasten off.

Left front

Re-join yarn to next 55 (**58**, 63, **68**, 72, **76**) sts keeping leopard pattern correct and working from chart.

Cont on these 55 (**58**, 63, **68**, 72, **76**) sts only in leopard pattern until work measures approx. 22 (**22**, 23⅝, **23⅝**, 25¼, **25¼**) in (56 (**56**, 60, **60**, 64, **64**) cm), ending with WS facing.

Next row (WS): Ch 2, work in leopard pattern over next 43 (**46**, 51, **56**, 60, **63**) sts, dc2tog twice, turn. *45 (**48**, 53, **58**, 62, **66**) sts*

Next row: Ch 2, dc2tog twice, work in leopard pattern over next 41 (**44**, 49, **54**, 58, **62**) sts, turn. *43 (**46**, 51, **56**, 60, **64**) sts*

Next row: Ch 2, work in leopard pattern over next 39 (**42**, 47, **52**, 56, **60**) sts, dc2tog twice, turn. *41 (**44**, 49, **54**, 58, **62**) sts*

Next row: Ch 2, dc2tog twice, work in leopard pattern over next 37 (**40**, 45, **50**, 54, **58**) sts, turn. *39 (**42**, 47, **52**, 56, **60**) sts*

Cont on these 39 (**42**, 47, **52**, 56, **60**) sts only, keeping leopard pattern correct, until work measures approx. 24½ (**24½**, 26, **26**, 27½, **27½**) in (62 (**62**, 66, **66**, 70, **70**) cm), ending with RS facing.

Fasten off.

Sleeves (make 2)

Using A, ch 80 (**80**, 87, **87**, 94, **94**).

Row 1 (RS): 1 sc in second ch from hook (skipped ch does not count as a st), 1 sc in every ch to end, turn. *79 (**79**, 86, **86**, 93, **93**) sts*

Row 2: Ch 1 (does not count as a st throughout), 1 sc in every st to end, turn.

Row 3: Ch 1, 1 dc in BLO of every st to end, turn.

Row 4: Ch 1, 1 dc in every st to end, turn.

Row 4 forms dc st.

Cont in dc st until sleeve measures approx. 12⅝ (**12⅝**, 13⅜, **14¼**, 15¾, **15¾**) in (32 (**32**, 34, **36**, 40, **40**) cm), ending with RS facing.

Fasten off.

Making up

Join shoulder seams.

Neckband
Using C, with RS facing and beg at Right Front neck, evenly place 20 sc up neck to shoulder seam, 36 sc across Back neck to left shoulder seam and 20 sc down Left Front neck.
Fasten off.

Front bands
Using C, with RS facing and beg at Right Front neck edge, evenly place 112 (**112**, 119, **119**, 126, **126**) sc to garment hem.
Fasten off.
Using C, with RS facing and beg at Left Front hem, evenly place 112 (**112**, 119, **119**, 126, **126**) sc up to neck edge.

Using preferred sewing up method, join center of last row on each sleeve to shoulder seam of body and sew sleeves in place approx. 8¾ (**8¾**, 9½, **9½**, 10¼, **10¼**) in (22 (**22**, 24, **24**, 26, **26**) cm) down each side of shoulder seam.
Rep for second sleeve.
Join sleeve and side seams.
Fasten off.

Weave in any loose ends. Press/block garment referring to ball band for instructions.

Tapestry intarsia technique

Carry any inactive yarn at the back of the work as foll:

1 Lay the inactive yarns over the hook at either the back (on a RS row) or at the front (on a WS row) once the hook is inserted into the stitch.

2 Pull up a loop, keeping the inactive yarn in the correct position.

3 Complete the stitch, taking all inactive yarn across the row. The correct yarn will then be in the right place when needed for changing color.

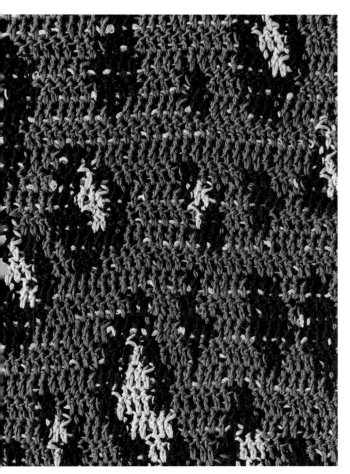
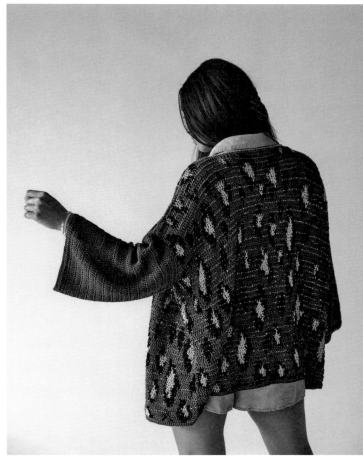

GINNY

Gingham Cardigan

Yet another modern take on an iconic pattern using crochet. This project will look amazing as gingham of any color or with contrast color sleeves—think mustard sleeves with a pale blue gingham, perhaps? The technique of laying inactive yarns inside the stitches creates a beautiful fabric inside and out and gives you such a neat and finished look.

Technique

Gingham tapestry crochet

Size

	Small	Medium	Large	XL	XXL	XXXL	
To fit	32–34	36–38	40–42	44–46	48–50	52–54	in
	81–86	91–96	101–106	112–117	122–127	132–137	cm
Actual	50	53⅛	57	61	65	72¾	in
	127	135	145	155	165	185	cm
Length	21¼	21¼	22	22¾	23⅝	24½	in
	54	54	56	58	60	62	cm
Sleeve length	17	17¾	18½	18½	19¼	19¼	in
	43	45	47	47	49	49	cm

* Model is wearing a size small.

Yarn

Worsted (aran)

Sample made in:

Debbie Bliss Cashmerino Aran (55% merino wool, 33% acrylic, 12% cashmere, 98 yd/ 90 m per 1¾ oz/50 g ball)

11 (**11**, 12, **13**, 14, **15**) balls of Black shade 300 (A)

6 (**7**, 8, **9**, 9, **10**) balls of White shade 25 (B)

3 (**4**, 4, **5**, 6, **7**) balls of Charcoal shade 28 (C)

Hook and Equipment

US 8 (5 mm) crochet hook
Yarn needle

Gauge (Tension)

16 sts x 8 rows to 4 x 4 in (10 x 10 cm) working gingham pattern, using US 8 (5 mm) crochet hook or size to obtain stated gauge.

Pattern Tip

When a new color is introduced, lay other colors over the hook toward the back of the work and trap inside each double crochet worked to trail non-used yarns across the row. Then when needed, pick up the new color and lay the old color behind as you did previously.

To work gingham intarsia you need to change colour before you finish working the previous st (see image 1, page 142), you then pull up loop with the new colour (see image 2, page 142) and then begin working the next st (see image 3 and 4, page 142) before repeating the process for the next 2 sts (see image 5, page 143).

MAKE

Back and fronts

Work in one piece to armholes.
Using A, ch 176 (**190**, 206, **222**, 238, **254**).
Row 1 (RS): 1 dc in third ch from hook (skipped ch do not count as a st), 1 dc in every ch to end, turn. *174 (**188**, 204, **220**, 236, **252**) sts*
Row 2: Ch 3 (does not count as a st throughout), *1 dc in next st, 1 BPdc in next st; rep from * to end, turn.
Row 3: Ch 3, *1 dc in A in BLO of next 2 sts, 1 dc in B in BLO of next 2 sts; rep from * to last 2 sts, 1 dc in A in BLO of last 2 sts, turn.
Row 4: Ch 3, *1 dc in B in next 2 sts, 1 dc in C in next 2 sts; rep from * to last 2 sts, 1 dc in B in last 2 sts, turn.
Row 5 (RS): Ch 3, *1 dc in A in next 2 sts, 1 dc in B in next 2 sts; rep from * to last 2 sts, 1 dc in A in last 2 sts, turn.
Row 6: Ch 3, *1 dc in B in next 2 sts, 1 dc in C in next 2 sts; rep from * to last 2 sts, 1 dc in B in last 2 sts, turn.
Rows 5 and 6 form gingham pattern.

Rep these 2 rows until work measures approx. 13⅜ (**13⅜**, 13¾, **14¼**, 15, **15⅜**) in (34 (**34**, 35, **36**, 38, **39**) cm), ending with RS facing.
Split for Front and Back.
Right front
Keep gingham pattern correct throughout.
Work straight in gingham pattern over next 36 (**40**, 44, **48**, 52, **52**) sts until work measures approx. 21¼ (**21¼**, 22, **22¾**, 23⅝, **24½**) in (54 (**54**, 56, **58**, 60, **62**) cm), ending with RS facing.
Fasten off.
Back
With RS facing, re-join yarn to next 102 (**108**, 116, **124**, 132, **148**) sts before split for Right Front and work gingham pattern in each of these 102 (**108**, 116, **124**, 132, **148**) sts, turn.
Now work straight in gingham pattern until work measures approx. 21¼ (**21¼**, 22, **22¾**, 23⅝, **24½**) in (54 (**54**, 56, **58**, 60, **62**) cm), ending with RS facing.
Fasten off.

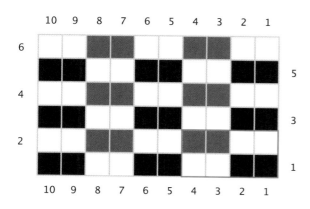

Key

- ☐ **RS** Knit **WS** Purl
- ■ **A** Black
- ☐ **B** White
- ▩ **C** Charcoal
- ☐ Pattern Repeat

5

Left front

With RS facing, re-join yarn to next 36 (**40**, 44, **48**, 52, **52**) sts left before split for Right Front and Back and work gingham pattern in each of these 36 (**40**, 44, **48**, 52, **52**) sts, turn.
Now work straight in gingham pattern until work measures approx. 21¼ (**21¼**, 22, **22¾**, 23⅝, **24½**) in (54 (**54**, 56, **58**, 60, **62**) cm), ending with RS facing.
Fasten off.

Sleeves (make 2)

Using A, ch 32 (**32**, 34, **36**, 36, **40**).
Row 1 (RS): 1 dc in third ch from hook (skipped ch do not count as a st), 1 dc in every ch to end, turn. *30 (**30**, 32, **34**, 34, **38**) sts*
Row 2: Ch 1 (does not count as a st throughout), 1 dc in every st to end, turn.
Now work straight in dc only (as set in last row) **WHILST** increasing by working 2 dc in first and last st of next and every alt row to 64 (**64**, 68, **70**, 70, **74**) sts.
Now work straight until sleeve measures approx. 17 (**17¾**, 18½, **18½**, 19¼, **19¼**) in (43 (**45**, 47, **47**, 49, **49**) cm), ending with RS facing.
Fasten off.

Making up

To join both shoulder seams, both Fronts will join to fasten-off row of Back leaving a 6¼ (**6¼**, 6¼, **7⅛**, 7⅛, **7⅞**) in (16 (**16**, 16, **18**, 18, **20**) cm) gap for Back neck. Join fasten-off row of each sleeve to shoulder seams and join each sleeve to garment body approx. 7⅞ (**7⅞**, 8¼, **8¾**, 8¾, **9**) in (20 (**20**, 21, **22**, 22, **23**) cm) down each side of shoulder seam. Join sleeve seams.

Front band

Using A and with RS of Right Front facing, evenly place 80 (**80**, 84, **86**, 88, **90**) sc up Right Front to shoulder seam, 18 (**18**, 18, **20**, 24, **26**) sc across Back neck, 80 (**80**, 84, **86**, 88, **90**) sc down Left Front back to beg ch. *178 (**178**, 186, **192**, 200, **206**) sts*
Next row (WS): Ch 3 (does not count as a st throughout), 1 dc in every st to end, turn.
Next row: Ch 3, *1 dc in next st, 1 FPdc in next st; rep from * to end, turn.
Fasten off.

Weave in any loose ends. Press/block garment referring to ball band for instructions.

AUDREY

Bobble and Ribbing Cardigan

A bobble and ribbing combo is a favorite of mine; I love how the line of bobbles frames the ribbing section and makes such a finished detail. The process of creating each bobble is also so therapeutic, and I enjoy each motion of wrapping the yarn round the hook before and after each stitch, too.

Technique

Working bobbles

Size

	Small	Medium	Large	XL	XXL	XXXL	
To fit	32–34	36–38	40–42	44–46	48–50	52–54	in
	81–86	91–96	101–106	112–117	122–127	132–137	cm
Actual	56¼	61	65¾	70½	75¼	80	in
	143	155	167	179	191	203	cm
Length	21¼	21⅝	22	22¾	23¼	23⅝	in
	54	55	56	58	59	60	cm
Sleeve length	17¾	17¾	18½	18½	19¼	19¼	in
	45	45	47	47	49	49	cm

* Model is wearing a size small.

Yarn

Bulky (chunky)
Sample made in:
Wool and the Gang Alpachino Merino (60% merino wool, 40% baby alpaca, 109 yd/ 100 m per 3½ oz/100 g ball)
11 (**12**, 12, **13**, 14, **15**) balls of Sahara Dust

Hook and Equipment

US 11 (8 mm) crochet hook
Yarn needle

Gauge (Tension)

11 sts x 7.5 rows to 4 x 4 in (10 x 10 cm) working half double ribbing, using US 11 (8 mm) crochet hook or size to obtain stated gauge.
10 sts x 12 rows to 4 x 4 in (10 x 10 cm) working single crochet, using US 11 (8 mm) crochet hook or size to obtain stated gauge.

Special Abbreviation

MB (make bobble): yo, insert hook into stitch, [yo, insert hook into same stitch, yo, pull up loop (3 loops on hook), yo, pull through two loops (see image 2, page 150)] 4 times, yo and pull through all loops, ch 1 (does not count as a st) to secure bobble (bobble made).

MAKE

Back and Fronts

Work in one piece to armholes.
Ch 32 (**33**, 33, **34**, 35, **35**).
Row 1 (RS): 1 hdc in second ch from hook (skipped ch does not count as a st), 1 hdc in every ch to end, turn. *31 (**32**, 32, **33**, 34, **34**) sts*
Row 2: Ch 1 (does not count as a st throughout), 1 hdc in BLO of every st to end, turn.
Rep Row 2 until work measures approx. 47¼ (**51¼**, 55⅛, **59**, 63, **67**) in (120 (**130**, 140, **150**, 160, **170**) cm), ending with RS facing.
With RS facing turn work at a 90-degree angle and begin to work down left-hand side of ribbing just made by evenly placing 143 (**155**, 167, **179**, 191, **203**) sts along edge to beg ch.
Next row (WS): Ch 1, 1 sc in every st to end, turn.
Next row: Ch 1, 1 sc in every st to end, turn.
Next row (bobbles): Ch 1, *1 sc in next st, MB in next st; rep from * to last st, 1 sc in last st, turn.
Next row: Ch 1, 1 sc in every st to end, turn.
Next row: Ch 1, 1 sc in every st to end, turn.
Split for Fronts and Back.

Right Front

Next row (RS): Ch 1, 1 sc in first st, sc2tog over next 2 sts, 1 sc in next 33 (**36**, 39, **42**, 45, **48**) sts, turn. *35 (**38**, 41, **44**, 47, **50**) sts*
Next row: Ch 1, 1 sc in every st to end, turn.
These 2 rows set Front neck shaping decreases every alt row over sc.
Cont as set decreasing every alt row 11 (**11**, 12, **13**, 13, **15**) times more, ending with RS facing. *24 (**27**, 29, **31**, 34, **35**) sts*
Medium, Large, XL, XXL and XXXL sizes only
Next row (RS): 1 sc in next – (**1**, 1, **1**, 1, **2**) sts, [1 sc in next – (**5**, 5, **3**, 3, **2**) sts, sc2tog] – (**3**, 3, **5**, 6, **7**) times, 1 sc in next – (**5**, 7, **5**, 3, **5**) sts. – (**24**, 26, **26**, 28, **28**) sts
Next row (WS): Ch 1, 1 sc in every st to end, turn.
All sizes
*24 (**24**, 26, **26**, 28, **28**) sts*
Fasten off.

Back

With RS facing, re-join yarn to next 71 (**77**, 83, **89**, 95, **101**) sts left before split for Right Front and work 1 sc in each of these 71 (**77**, 83, **89**, 95, **101**) sts, turn.

Next row (WS): Ch 1, 1 sc in every st to end, turn.

Now work straight in sc as set in last row until armhole measures approx. 7⅞ (**7⅞**, 8¼, **8¾**, 8¾, **9½**) in (20 (**20**, 21, **22**, 22, **24**) cm), ending with RS facing.

Next row (RS): Ch 1, 1 sc in next 27 (**27**, 29, **32**, 34, **37**) sts, sc2tog over next 2 sts, turn. *28 (**28**, 30, **33**, 35, **38**) sts*

Next row (WS): 1 sc in next 4 (**4**, 5, **6**, 7, **4**) sts, [1 sc in next 3 (**3**, 3, **1**, 1, **1**) sts, sc2tog] 4 (**4**, 5, **7**, 7, **10**) times, 1 sc in next 4 (**4**, 1, **6**, 7, **4**) sts. *24 (**24**, 26, **26**, 28, **28**) sts*

Next row: Ch 1, 1 sc in every st to end, turn. Fasten off.

Note: Armhole should measure approx. 8¾ (**8¾**, 9, **9½**, 9½, **9¾**) in (22 (**22**, 23, **24**, 24, **25**) cm) from split.

Skip center sts for neckband and re-join yarn to last 29 (**29**, 31, **34**, 36, **39**) sts as foll:

Next row (RS): Ch 1, sc2tog over first 2 sts, 1 sc in next 27 (**27**, 29, **32**, 34, **37**) sts, turn. *28 (**28**, 30, **33**, 35, **38**) sts*

Next row (WS): 1 sc in next 4 (**4**, 5, **6**, 7, **4**) sts, [1 sc in next 3 (**3**, 3, **1**, 1, **1**) sts, sc2tog] 4 (**4**, 5, **7**, 7, **10**) times, 1 sc in next 4 (**4**, 1, **6**, 7, **4**) sts. *24 (**24**, 26, **26**, 28, **28**) sts*

Fasten off.

Note: Armhole should measure approx. 7⅞ (**7⅞**, 8¼, **8¾**, 8¾, **9**) in (20 (**20**, 21, **22**, 22, **23**) cm) from split.

Left front

With RS facing, re-join yarn to next 36 (**39**, 83, **89**, 95, **101**) sts left before split for Right Front and Back and work as foll:

Next row (RS): Ch 1, 1 sc in next 33 (**36**, 39, **42**, 45, **48**) sts, sc2tog over next 2 sts, 1 sc last st, turn. *35 (**38**, 41, **44**, 47, **50**) sts*

Next row: Ch 1, 1 sc in every st to end, turn.

These 2 rows set front neck shaping decreases on every alt row over sc.

Cont as set, decreasing every alt row 11 (**11**, 12, **13**, 13, **15**) times more, ending with RS facing. *24 (**27**, 29, **31**, 34, **35**) sts*

Medium, Large, XL, XXL and XXXL sizes only

Next row (RS): 1 sc in next – (**1**, 1, **1**, 1, **2**) sts, [1 sc in next – (**5**, 5, **3**, 3, **2**) sts, sc2tog] – (**3**, 3, **5**, 6, **7**) times, 1 sc in next – (**5**, 7, **5**, 3, **5**) sts. *– (**24**, 26, **26**, 28, **28**) sts*

Next row (WS): Ch 1, 1 sc in every st to end, turn.

All sizes

*24 (**24**, 26, **26**, 28, **28**) sts*

Fasten off.

Sleeves (make 2)

Ch 40 (**42**, 44, **44**, 46, **46**).
Row 1 (RS): 1 hdc in second ch from hook (skipped ch does not count as a st), 1 hdc in every ch to end, turn. *39 (**41**, 43, **43**, 45, **45**) sts*
Row 2: Ch 1 (does not count as a st throughout), 1 hdc in BLO of every st to end, turn.
Rep Row 2 until work measures approx. 15¾ (**15¾**, 16½, **17¼**, 17¼, **18⅛**) in (40 (**40**, 42, **44**, 44, **46**) cm), ending with RS facing.
With RS facing turn work at a 90-degree angle and begin to work down left-hand side of ribbing just made by evenly placing 44 (**44**, 46, **48**, 48, **50**) sts along edge to beg ch.
Next row (WS): Ch 1, 1 sc in every st to end, turn.
Next row: Ch 1, 1 sc in every st to end, turn.
Next row (bobbles): Ch 1, *1 sc in next st, MB in next st; rep from * to last st, 1 sc in last st, turn.
Now work straight in sc only until sleeve measures approx. 17¾ (**17¾**, 18½, **18½**, 19¼, **19¼**) in (45 (**45**, 47, **47**, 49, **49**) cm), ending with WS facing.
Fasten off.

Making up

Join both shoulder seams. Join the center of the last row of single crochet on each sleeve to the shoulder seams and join each sleeve to the garment body approx. 7⅞ (**7⅞**, 8¼, **8¾**, 8¾, **9**) in (20 (**20**, 21, **22**, 22, **23**) cm) down each side of the shoulder seam. Join each side and sleeve seam.

Cuffs

Using a long length of yarn work running st around edge of sleeve cuff, then pull in so cuff measures approx. 7⅞ (**7⅞**, 8¼, **8¾**, 8¾, **9**) in (20 (**20**, 21, **22**, 22, **23**) cm).
Fasten off.
Now evenly place 24 (**24**, 26, **28**, 28, **30**) sc around edging of cuff, sl st into first sc made to form rounds.
Next round: Ch 1 (does not count as a st), 1 sc in every st to end, sl st into first sc made.
Fasten off.
Rep for second cuff.

Front band

With RS of Right Front facing, evenly place 68 (**69**, 70, **73**, 74, **75**) sc up Right Front to shoulder seam, 23 (**23**, 25, **25**, 27, **27**) sc across Back neck, and 68 (**69**, 70, **73**, 74, **75**) sc down Left Front back to beg ch. 159 (**161**, 165, **171**, 175, **177**) sc
Next row (WS): Ch 1 (does not count as a st throughout), 1 sc in every st to end, turn.
Next row: Ch 1, 1 sc in every st to end, turn.
Fasten off.

Weave in any loose ends. Press/block garment referring to ball band for instructions.

BLANK MODELS

Experiment by creating your
own colorways for sweater,
cardigans and accessory designs
using the principles in this book.

I can't wait to see what you
make from this book. Please
use the hashtag #emmacrocheted
to share snaps of your creations
on Instagram.

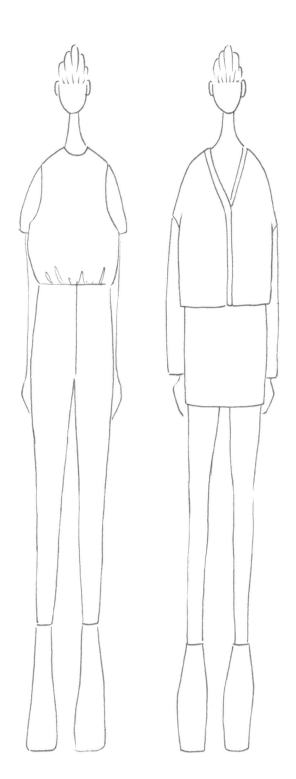

ACKNOWLEDGMENTS

I want to begin by saying a big thank you to Quadrille Publishing whose continued support and encouragement has led to this book, especially to Harriet Butt, my commissioning editor. Your time, support and patience are highly appreciated and of course your baby-occupying duties on the shoot. A big thank you to Katherine Keeble for yet another stunning book design, and to Kim Lightbody, whose amazing photography captures my designs in the best possible light.

To my wonderful makers, Cheryl, Sarah and Gwen as well as my Nan June for brushing off her hooks to help me meet my deadlines and always supporting and believing in me. I would also like to thank the wonderful models, Megan McWhire, Paige Drury-Lawrence and Lucia Herbert for wearing my designs so beautifully, and to Rachael Keeley for such stunning hair and make-up. I'd also love to thank Charlotte Melling for out-of-this-world styling and to Marie for perfectly editing and proofreading my patterns.

I'd also love to thank the amazing companies who have supported my career so far and have generously given me the yarn support for the garments in this book; Love Crafts, Debbie Bliss, Wool and the Gang, Rico, The fibre co, Rowan, Sirdar, Erika Knight and Britta at Selected Yarns.

I cannot begin to thank my family enough for their continued support, especially my mum and dad who have always championed me in everything I do. I am fortunate to have such supportive grandparents and an extremely patient sister who often proofreads my writing. I would also love to thank the rest of my amazing family who have all encouraged and helped me along my journey to creating this book. Last but most certainly not least, thank you to my husband Lewis who encourages and inspires me daily, along with our beautiful children Max and Imogen, who I thank for taking the occasional extra-long nap so I could finish this book!

ABOUT THE AUTHOR

Emma Wright is a fashion, knit and crochet designer. She is heavily influenced by color and floral patterns, which is reflected through the playfulness of her designs.

Sine graduating in 2014, she has turned emmaknitted into a full-time business, designing knit and crochet patterns for yarn brands and magazines in the industry. Emma was subsequently awarded the coveted 'Britain Next Top Knitwear Designer' by Lovecrafts. Emma lives just outside of Sheffield with her husband, Lewis, and children, Max and Imogen.

@emmaknitted

Publishing Director
Sarah Lavelle

Senior Commissioning Editor
Harriet Butt

Assistant Editor
Oreolu Grillo

Design and Art Direction
Katherine Keeble

Stylist
Charlotte Melling

Photographer
Kim Lightbody

Make Up Artist
Rachael Keeley

Models
Megan McWhire, Lucia Herbert
and Paige Drury-Lawrence

Head of Production
Stephen Lang

Senior Production Controller
Lisa Fiske, Gary Hayes

Published in 2022 by Quadrille,
an imprint of Hardie Grant
Publishing

Quadrille
52–54 Southwark Street
London SE1 1UN
quadrille.com

Cataloguing in Publication Data:
a catalogue record for this book is
available from the British Library.

text and patterns © Emma Wright
2023
photography © Kim Lightbody 2023
design © Quadrille 2023

ISBN 978 1 78713 868 1

Printed using soy inks in China

FSC
www.fsc.org

MIX
Paper from
responsible sources
FSC™ C020056